The Spanish Inq

D0686358

Historical Association Studies

General Editors: Muriel Chamberlain, H. T. Dickinson and Joe Smith

Published Titles

Forthcoming Titles

† Print on demand
* Out of print

The Historical Association, founded in 1906, brings together people who share an interest in, and love for, the past. It aims to further the study and teaching of history at all levels: teacher and student, amateur and professional. This is one of over 100 publications available at preferential rates to members. Membership also includes journals at generous discounts and gives access to courses, conferences, tours and regional and local activities. Full details are available from The Secretary, The Historical Association, 59a Kennington Park Road, London SE11 4JH, telephone: 020 7735 3901.

The Spanish Inquisition

Helen Rawlings

Blackwell
Publishing

BLACKWELL PUBLISHING
350 Main Street, Malden, MA 02148-5020, USA
9600 Garsington Road, Oxford OX4 2DQ, UK
550 Swanston Street, Carlton, Victoria 3053, Australia

First published 2006 by Blackwell Publishing Ltd

3   2007

Library of Congress Cataloging-in-Publication Data

Rawlings, Helen
  The Spanish Inquisition / Helen Rawlings.
    p. cm.—(Historical Association studies)
Includes bibliographical references and index.
ISBN 978-0-631-20599-9 (hardcover : alk. paper) — ISBN 978-0-631-20600-2 (pbk. : alk. paper) 1. Inquisition—Spain. 2. Spain—Church history. I. Title. II. Series.

BX1735.R39 2005
272'.2'0946—dc22

2004008968

A catalogue record for this title is available from the British Library.

Set in 10.5/12.5 Times
by Kolam Information Services Pvt. Ltd, Pondicherry, India.
Printed and bound in India
by Replika Press Pvt. Ltd

The publisher's policy is to use permanent paper from mills that operate a sustainable forestry policy, and which has been manufactured from pulp processed using acid-free and elementary chlorine-free practices. Furthermore, the publisher ensures that the text paper and cover board used have met acceptable environmental accreditation standards.

For further information on
Blackwell Publishing, visit our website:
www.blackwellpublishing.com

For John Lynch

Contents

Contents   ix

Maps and Plates

Map

Plates

Acknowledgements

The author and publisher gratefully acknowledge the permission granted to reproduce the copyright material in this book:

Material from chapters 1 and 2 of my *Church, Religion and Society in Early Modern Spain* (Palgrave, 2002) has been reproduced with kind permission of Palgrave Macmillan.

Drawings by Francisco de Goya have been reproduced with kind permission of the Museo del Prado, Madrid (Plates 7.1, 7.2, 7.3, 7.5 and 7.6) and the British Museum, London (Plate 7.4).

Every effort has been made to trace copyright holders and to obtain their permission for the use of copyright material. The publisher apologizes for any errors or omissions in the above list and would be grateful if notified of any corrections that should be incorporated in future reprints or editions of this book.

Chronology

1640   Tribunal of Inquisition established in Madrid to deal with Portuguese crypto-Jews.

1665   Reign of Charles II begins.

1680   *Auto de fe* in Madrid against Portuguese crypto-Jews.

1700   Reign of Philip V begins.

1720s   Renewal of trials of Judaizers in Castile.

1746   Reign of Ferdinand VI begins.

1759   Reign of Charles III begins.

1767   Proposals announced to reduce authority of Inquisition. Expulsion of Jesuits from Spain.

1776   Pablo de Olavide, enlightened minister of Charles III, charged with heresy.

1788   Reign of Charles IV begins.

1789   French Revolution breaks out.

1797   Goya's *Caprichos.*

1798   Gaspar de Jovellanos attacks Inquisition in paper addressed to king.

1808   War of Independence/Peninsular War begins. Charles IV deposed.
        Joseph Bonaparte announces suppression of Inquisition.

1813   Cortes of Cádiz votes to abolish the Inquisition.

1814   War of Independence ends. Restoration of Inquisition by Ferdinand VII.

c.1816 Goya's *Tribunal of the Inquisition.*

1817   Publication of Llorente's *Historia crítica de la Inquisición española.*

1820   Ferdinand VII, under liberal pressure, suppresses Inquisition.

1834   Permanent abolition of the Inquisition by Isabella II.

1865   Abolition of Statutes of Purity of Blood.

1 The Historiography of the Inquisition

Introduction

The Inquisition was one of the most powerful and polemical institutions used by the Roman Catholic Church to eliminate heresy and protect the unity of Christendom. Although tribunals were operative in Bohemia, France and Italy in medieval times, it is the Spanish Inquisition – first established in the kingdom of Castile in 1478 under Queen Isabella I and suppressed 356 years later in 1834 under Queen Isabella II – which has left its mark on the whole history of western civilization. While sharing many features of the Aragonese tribunal set up to deal with the threat of Catharism emanating from French territories in the thirteenth century, the Spanish Inquisition was different in one fundamental respect: it was responsible to the Crown rather than the Pope and was used to consolidate state interest. It soon acquired a reputation for being a barbarous, repressive instrument of racial and religious intolerance that regularly employed torture as well as the death penalty as punishments and severely restricted Spain's intellectual development for generations. The rigours of the Inquisition gave rise to the so-called 'Black Legend' – an image of Spain as a nation of fanatical bigots, that was popularized by her foreign (mainly Protestant) enemies in the mid-sixteenth century, and which survived long after the tribunal's final extinction.

Given the controversy surrounding its existence and reputation, the Spanish Inquisition has generated an enormous volume of historical literature. This has been shaped over the centuries by a number of factors. These include the political, social and ideological viewpoints of scholars, their access to and interpretation of relevant sources and the climate of the age in which they were written. Beyond being simply a historical phenomenon, the Inquisition has become a historiographical phenomenon, forging a number of 'schools' and 'generations'. Historians have traditionally looked at the institution from a variety of perspectives. Those approaches that predominate are: its persecution of minority faiths in the name of orthodoxy; its political role as a tool of the authoritarian state; the amount of corruption, torture and prejudice that underpinned its activities; the support and opposition it generated in society; and the extent to which it contributed to Spain's political, cultural and economic decline. In terms of its overall reputation, observers have tended to divide sharply in their judgements. For some liberal writers it was an expression of all that was 'bad' about the autocratic regime that ruled Spain for generations, while for others of more conservative persuasion it represented all that was 'good'.

Since the mid-1970s, a new school of historians have examined the institution afresh from more objective multi-disciplinary standpoints that have challenged the findings of traditional scholarship. For example, it is now acknowledged that the Spanish Inquisition was a far less repressive instrument of ideological control than had hitherto been thought, and that torture and the death penalty were only rarely applied – almost exclusively during the first two decades of its existence. By comparison, other European countries, including England, France and Germany, continued to burn heretics until well into the seventeenth century. Furthermore, the Spanish Inquisition was not solely concerned with the pursuit of religious minorities: a significant part of its work involved interacting with ordinary Spaniards in the local context, correcting aspects of their behaviour and belief. Nor was the Holy Office as powerful an institution as previously envisaged. In practice it had to accommodate itself to the jurisdiction of other organs of government, as well as to that of the Church and the Crown. It frequently wrestled with conflicts of authority within its own ranks. This chapter will look at the changing trends in our perception of the Spanish Inquisition over five hundred years of history.

Sixteenth- and Seventeenth-century Literature

From the middle of the fifteenth century, prior to the establishment of the Spanish Inquisition, polemical literature was being
published which stirred up anti-semitic tensions in society. Some
of it was generated by the descendants of Jews who had converted to Christianity (known as *conversos*) and sought to dis-
tance themselves from the beliefs of their forefathers. Pablo de
Santa María, Archbishop of Burgos (1415–35), figured among
them. He wrote a tract in 1432 (*Scrutinium scripturarum*) in
which he criticized those Jews who stubbornly resisted conversion. Much more controversial and racist in tone was Alonso de
Espina's book, *Fortalitium fidei contra Judaeos*, published in
1460. In it the Franciscan friar detailed the transgressions of
conversos (including their observance of Jewish rites and fake
compliance with Christian ones) and called for legal action to be
taken against those found guilty of such practices. His proposals
were later to serve as a blueprint for the policy of the Spanish
Inquisition (Beinart, 1981, pp. 9–20). By contrast, Friar Alonso
de Oropesa, the general of the Jeronimites (a late medieval order
of friars), advocated the tolerance and education of *converso*
heretics in his *Lumen ad revelationem gentium* of 1465, an attitude supported by the Archbishop of Toledo, Alfonso Carrillo
(1466–82) (Kamen, 1997, pp. 33–5).

When the Spanish Inquisition began its operations in 1480, it
aroused a variety of responses. The contemporary historian and
local Andalusian priest, Andrés Bernáldez, in his chronicle,
Memorias del reinado de los Reyes Católicos, completed by
1509, justified the need for the tribunal from a characteristically
zealous Old Christian perspective (i.e. that of a Christian by
birth). He recorded that over 700 converted Jews had been
burnt and more than 5,000 punished at the hands of the Sevillian
Inquisition by 1488 and triumphantly declared that 'the heretics
of Córdoba, Toledo, Burgos, Valencia and Segovia, and the
whole of Spain were discovered to be all Jews [...] Since the
fire is lit it will burn until [...] not one of those who judaized is
left' (Bernáldez, 1962, pp. 102–3, 251). On the other hand, Fernando del Pulgar, secretary to the Catholic kings and a New

Christian by birth (i.e. a convert to Christianity of Jewish or Muslim descent), took a more sympathetic stance. In correspondence with the Archbishop of Seville, Don Pedro González de Mendoza, in the early 1480s, Pulgar criticized the cruel activity of the Inquisition in Seville. While agreeing that *conversos* who continued to practise their old faith should not be tolerated, he argued against persecution, advocating that persuasive, educative methods should be adopted to bring them back into the Christian fold: 'To burn them would be an extremely cruel and difficult act and would force them to flee in desperation to places where no correction would ever be expected of them' (Cantera Burgos, 1972, p. 308; Beinart, 1981, pp. 36–9). His was not an isolated view. Friar Hernando de Talavera, confessor to Queen Isabella, was another influential dissenting voice. He advocated in his *Católica impugnación* of 1487 that 'neither the Jew nor the Moor should be punished for keeping their faith [. . .] nor should they be forced to adhere to the Catholic faith' (Fernández de Madrid, 1992, p. lvi). Such controversial opinions, many voiced from within the Church itself, were probably more widespread than the historical evidence suggests but were silenced for political reasons.

The Black Legend

The term 'Black Legend' is, surprisingly, of recent origin, attributed to the Spanish journalist Julián Juderías, in an essay written in 1912. It refers to an attitude that was prevalent in northern European thinking in the second half of the sixteenth century when international criticism of the Inquisition began to emerge in those countries politically and ideologically opposed to Spain. Protestant pamphleteers in the Netherlands, German states, England and France vigorously promoted its savage reputation via the printing press. The legend, some of it generated by Spanish Protestant exiles, was designed to promulgate the blackest facts about Spain and its rulers to serve as a warning of the consequences of Spanish hegemony in Europe. Accordingly, Spain became synonymous with all forms of repression, brutality, religious and political intolerance, as well as with intellectual and artistic backwardness. The Spanish conquest of America helped to advance the legend, drawing upon the shameful, barbarous treatment of native Amerindians by the conquistadors, as documented by contemporary observers. Bartolomé de Las Casas was perhaps the most outspoken critic of Spanish colonialism in the New World. In his *Brief Account of the Destruction of the Indies* of 1542, he described with great passion the atrocities committed by Spaniards against innocent Indians and prophesied that the conquering nation would itself decline as a result.

Among the most critical accounts of the work of the Inquisition written outside Spain was that of the English Protestant John Foxe. Drawing upon Las Casas' condemnation of Spanish brutality, he exaggerated the Holy Office's repressive practices so as to propagate anti-Catholic opinion. In his *Book of Martyrs* of 1554, he wrote of 'the extreme dealing and cruel ravening of these Catholic Inquisitors of Spain, who, under the pretended visor of religion, do nothing but seek their private gain and commodity, with crafty defrauding and spoiling of other men's goods' (Maltby, 1971, p. 35). The work that had most influence on the propagation of the Black Legend was *Sanctae Inquisitionis Hispanicae Artes* (*A Discovery and Plaine Declaration of sundry Subtill Practices of the Holy Inquisition of Spain*) written by the pseudonymous author Reginaldus Gonsalvius Montanus (most likely a Protestant Spaniard who had been associated with Lutheran activity in Seville). The book describes the cruel procedures of the Inquisition in graphic detail. It was published in Heidelberg in 1567 in Latin and was soon reprinted in several languages. The wide dissemination of the text was to be a major contributory factor to the persistence of anti-Spanish and anti-Inquisition propaganda in Protestant northern Europe for close on four centuries (Kinder, 1997, pp. 75–6).

Eighteenth- and Nineteenth-century Literature

It was not until the beginning of the nineteenth century that the lid was lifted on the Inquisition from the inside. Juan Antonio Llorente worked first as a fiscal secretary to the bishop of

Burgos, then as a commissioner for the tribunal of the Inquisition located in Logroño (1785), and subsequently as secretary of the Supreme Council of Inquisition (the *Suprema*) in Madrid (1788). In the 1790s he entered the service of Manuel Godoy, the enlightened minister of Charles IV, whose political persuasions he shared, and began writing a series of essays on the reform of the Holy Office which won him favours at court. He used the opportunity afforded by the French invasions of Spain (1808–14) and the liberal reforms that followed (including the temporary abolition of the Holy Office) to write a 'true' history of the Inquisition, based on his own experience and access to its archives. In 1813, on the return of Ferdinand VII to the Spanish throne and the revival of the Holy Office, he left for France where he wrote his most celebrated work, *Historia crítica de la Inquisición española (Critical History of the Spanish Inquisition)* published in Paris in 1817. It was soon translated into several languages, including Spanish in 1822. Llorente pointed to the failure of the Church to provide *conversos* and *moriscos* (Jewish and Moorish converts to Christianity) with adequate religious instruction as a factor that led them to revert to the practice of their old faith. 'The Inquisition maintained and strengthened its hypocrisy, punishing only those who knew no better; but it converted nobody. The Jews and Moors were baptised without proper conversion', he wrote (Llorente, 1980, I, p. 8). He criticized the Inquisition for inhibiting the development of the arts, industry and trade, and condemned inquisitors for being motivated by financial greed rather than religious uniformity. Llorente, despite the bad press he received in Spain (leading to his excommunication from the Catholic Church in 1823), nevertheless captured some of the discrepancies inherent in the Inquisition's evolution, acknowledged by many of his contemporaries. Essentially he felt that the institution had exceeded the limits of its authority and that its powers should now be returned to the Crown and the Church. Llorente's study was to have a major impact on nineteenth-century historiography, provoking both supportive and defensive reactions. Its publication coincided with the beginning of the Inquisition's demise as an institution and may even have hastened it (García-Cárcel and Moreno Martínez, 2000, pp. 95–101). Despite the tight grip exercised by the Inquisition in matters of censorship, criticisms of the institution circulated freely both inside and outside Spain. The American historian William Prescott in his *History of the Reign of Ferdinand and Isabella* (1837) followed Llorente's line of argument by drawing attention to the destructive, repressive force of the Inquisition, deeming it to be responsible for 'centuries of unspeakable oppression and misery' (Prescott, 1854, p. 292).

Llorente apart, the majority of nineteenth-century Spanish historians of the Inquisition were members of the secular clergy or the religious orders studying the tribunal of the faith from a Catholic perspective and a Tridentine mentality. They included José Amador de los Ríos who saw the Inquisition as ultimately serving justifiable political ends (1848) and Orti y Lara who supported the Inquisition's crusade against heresy as inspired by God and essential to the preservation of Spain's national identity (1877). Marcelino Menéndez y Pelayo in his *Historia de los heterodoxos españoles* (1880–2) maintained that the Spanish Inquisition was a fundamental instrument of the Catholic state. By separating out the faithful from the unfaithful it strengthened the religious unity of the Spanish kingdoms and, by extension, their political cohesion (Menéndez y Pelayo, 1992, I, p. 894). These theories were suitably adapted for propaganda purposes by the Franco regime in the mid-twentieth century in the crusade it led against the enemies of Fascism.

The transfer of the archives of the Spanish Inquisition from Simancas, near Valladolid, to the Archivo Histórico Nacional in Madrid at the beginning of the twentieth century (1914), and their subsequent re-cataloguing, marked a further turning point in the development of the institution's history. It facilitated scholars' access to extensive archival evidence, studied by only a select few up to this juncture, including the American historian Henry Charles Lea. In his monumental four-volume *A History of the Inquisition of Spain* (1922), Lea challenged the apologetic approach of much traditional Spanish scholarship to produce a detailed, critical study of the institution's role and influence. Lea's work was, not surprisingly, fiercely condemned by traditionalists, including the Jesuit historian Bernardino Llorca, and was not published in Spanish until 1982–4. Despite the considerable advances in inquisitorial research made by Lea, as well as by other contemporary foreign scholars, including Ernest Shäfer in 1902–3 and Marcel Bataillon in 1937, until the middle of the twentieth century the Spanish Inquisition continued to be examined by native historians from predominantly conservative perspectives as an institution dedicated to the suppression of Jewish, Islamic and Protestant heresies. It was not until the death of General Franco in 1975 that the history of the Inquisition began to be treated with greater objectivity and impartiality by Spanish scholars, free from the 'politicization' that had dominated nineteenth- and twentieth-century scholarship. It is highly significant that this flourishing of revisionist inquisitorial historiography has coincided with Spain's own process of political and social democratization.

Twentieth-century Scholarship

Detailed research carried out since the late 1970s by a new generation of international scholars has fundamentally challenged the traditional approach to inquisitorial scholarship and prompted a thorough reappraisal of its role. Where British scholarship is concerned, Professor Henry Kamen stimulated this sea change in his pioneering *The Spanish Inquisition* (1965) which exploded the myth surrounding the Black Legend. Twenty years later he updated his findings in *Inquisition and Society in Spain in the Sixteenth and Seventeenth Centuries* (1985), offering a revised summary of the advances in inquisitorial research. His latest contribution, *The Spanish Inquisition: An Historical Revision* (1997), adds the findings of the most recent scholarship. Kamen emphasizes the multi-faceted nature of the institution and its marginal impact on civil liberties. Although it was established with a specific jurisdiction over converted Jews, it soon acquired the power to enquire into the behaviour of any Christian man or woman, dead or alive. Inquisitors' definition of heresy became subject to multiple interpretations of a social, moral, cultural and ideological nature. What interested them was how far the accused deviated from the orthodox norms of social acceptability rather than what he or she thought or believed. The Inquisition came to mirror the broad realities of time and place, accommodating itself to different needs and circumstances across the Spanish regions. According to Kamen's thesis, this is what enabled it to survive for over 350 years.

Differing points of view have emerged among twentieth-century Jewish historians of the Inquisition. Benzion Netanyahu, in his controversial work *The Origins of the Inquisition* (1995), saw the reason for its establishment in purely anti-semitic terms. According to his viewpoint the Crown was racially motivated in setting up the Holy Office and concealed its prejudices by exaggerating the numbers of crypto-Jews, the majority of whom were actually sincere Christians. On the other hand, Haim Beinart in *Records of the Trials of the Spanish Inquisition in Ciudad Real, 1483–1485* (1974) and Yitzhak Baer in *A History of the Jews in Christian Spain* (1961) both affirmed that the Inquisition was set up to resolve a specific socio-religious problem created by the expansion of the *converso* class and was not anti-semitic in nature. In their view, inquisitors were correct to regard *conversos* as Judaizers, many of whom continued to practise their former faith in secret.

The work of modern historians, including Jean-Pierre Dedieu's *L'Administration de la Foi. L'Inquisition de Tolède, xvie–xviiie siècle* (1989), Sara Nalle's *God in La Mancha. Religious Reform and the People of Cuenca, 1500–1650* (1992), Stephen Haliczer's *Inquisition and Society in Early Modern Europe* (1987a) and Bartolomé Bennassar's *L'Inquisition Espagnole, xv–xix siècle* (1979), has revealed the important contribution that inquisitorial sources are able to make to the social and cultural history of Spain. Each defendant was subjected to a rigorous interrogation upon arrest. They had to provide details of their family background, occupation, level of literacy and the circumstances surrounding their accusation (which might include reference to moral behaviour and superstitious practices). Following the Council of Trent (1545–63), which established a wide-ranging programme for reform within the Catholic Church, the Inquisition became concerned about the level of religious instruction of the people and incorporated a test of doctrinal knowledge into its interrogation procedures. From the mid-sixteenth century it became a kind of 'teaching machine'. Via the edict of faith (the public announcement of crimes of heresy) and the *auto de fe* (the public denunciation of those accused of heresy) it set out a code of accepted practice for Catholics on matters of sexuality, blasphemy, magic and sorcery. Defendants were required to recite the four basic Church prayers, make the sign of the cross and confirm the regularity of their attendance at communion and confession. The analysis of this carefully recorded information has led to a number of fascinating studies into the culture, belief and mentality of Old Christian Spanish society in the early modern period. The following example (a declaration made before the tribunal of Toledo by a construction worker, Antonio Márquez, aged 25) tells us about the principal pattern of a Spaniard's life, his geographical and professional mobility, childhood experiences and adult education:

> I was born at La Solana and raised in my father's house until age ten. It was there I learned to read and write ... I've been a choir boy in my village. At that age I went with my father to the kingdom of Valencia, in the service of Mosen Guillén, a cleric, for three years. From there I returned to my village and stayed there five or six years, working with my father. Then I went off to the kingdom of Murica, to Orihuela, nearly six months, learning the craft of bricklayer. I next went to Madrid, where I stayed three or four months, working at my trade on the king's projects; then to Toledo, and next to Valencia with a merchant named Pedro de Valencia, and Alonso Alvarez, another merchant, son of Antonio Alvarez Díaz, with whom I remained two years, always travelling. Then I moved to Segovia and, since I was not well, I returned after spending a month and a half there. Then I worked on the King's projects at Aravaca, from whence I returned to Toledo, where I am now living with a certain Tapia, and from where I was taken as a prisoner to the Holy Office. (Dedieu, 1986, p. 165)

We now have a more detailed knowledge of the diversity of practice that characterized the Spanish Inquisition at regional level from a number of recent studies made of its provincial tribunals. The activity of the Valencian Holy Office, studied in detail by Ricardo García-Cárcel in *Orígenes de la Inquisición española. El tribunal de Valencia, 1478–1530* (1976) and *Herejía y sociedad en el siglo xvi. La Inquisición en Valencia, 1530–1609*

(1980), can be divided into two distinct phases. From its foundation until 1530 it tried about 2,350 people, 90 per cent of whom were *conversos* suspected of being backsliding Jews. Seven hundred and fifty of them were put to death for their crimes. Between 1530 and 1609, the tribunal brought around 4,250 defendants to trial. Over two-thirds of them were *moriscos*, of whom 24 suffered the death penalty. The tribunal of Santiago in north-west Galicia, the subject of a study by Jaime Contreras, *El Santo Oficio de la Inquisición de Galicia: poder, sociedad y cultura* (1982), dealt with a very different clientele from that of Valencia. Originally established in 1574 to combat the supposed Protestant menace along Spain's remote north coast, it prosecuted foreign heretics, including Lutherans and Portuguese *conversos*, but also Galicians themselves, charged with the lesser offences of blasphemy and bigamy. In the seventeenth century, both institutions underwent change. In the case of Valencia, it rose in status, while that of Santiago became more peripheral in standing and riddled with corruption.

In *Frontiers of Heresy: The Spanish Inquisition from the Basque Lands to Sicily* (1990), William Monter explores the institutional development of all those tribunals governed by the Aragonese Secretariat (Zaragoza, Navarre, Barcelona, Valencia and Sicily), created in 1517 and abolished in 1618. Opposition to the Holy Office was intense in the Aragonese lands, particularly among the political elite who feared its impingement upon their local laws known as *fueros* and therefore their ability to govern themselves with minimal royal interference (Monter, 1990, p. 321). Monter maintains that an appreciation of the essential differences between the Aragonese and the Castilian Inquisitions (beyond the formality of their bureaucratic separation) is essential for a proper understanding of the history of the Spanish Inquisition. He argues that, with the decline of Jewish and Protestant persecutions in Castile from mid-century, the geographical focus of inquisitorial activity shifted to the Crown of Aragón. From 1570 the Aragonese Inquisition extended its jurisdiction over a variety of offences not commonly pursued or encountered in Castile. Its most prominent victims were *moriscos*, and foreign immigrants suspected of Lutheranism as well as those accused of witchcraft and sodomy. By avoiding disciplining the Old

Christian community for crimes such as blasphemy, superstition and ignorance in matters of the faith, as was the custom in Castile, and concentrating instead on marginal elements of local society, the Aragonese Inquisition gained the 'political' support and respect of their quasi-autonomous subjects. According to Monter, it thus became 'a respected agent of royal authority'. It also gained a reputation for the harshness of its punishments: 2 per cent of victims of the Aragonese tribunals were condemned to death in person as compared to 1.6 per cent in Castile between 1540 and 1700. Most of these deaths occurred at the height of its activity between 1570 and 1625 (Monter, 1990, pp. 48–9). Following the expulsion of the *moriscos* (1609–14) the work of the Holy Office declined in Aragón and from 1625 the Castilian Inquisition again regained its primacy (Monter, 1990, pp. xii–xiii). The activity of the Inquisition was thus conditional upon the prevailing social and political climates in Castile and Aragón and to some extent reflects the balance of power between the centre and the periphery.

The Inquisitorial Data-bank

One of the most significant advances in inquisitorial research in recent decades has been carried out by the Danish ethnographer-historian Gustav Henningsen, and the Spanish scholar Jaime Contreras. In 1972 Henningsen and Contreras embarked upon a quantitative study of almost 50,000 summaries of trial records (*relaciones de causas*) – classified according to types of crime committed – of the 21 regional tribunals of the Spanish Inquisition over the period 1540–1700 to produce a statistical 'data-bank' of its activities (see table 1.1). Their systematic analysis of the evidence has revealed a number of important new perspectives on its history. First, the Inquisition was nowhere near as bloodthirsty and repressive an instrument of ideological control as commonly perceived. The holocausts of the 1480s were short-lived. For most of its active history the execution rate remained below 2 per cent – an average of five people per year. Torture and the death penalty were only rarely applied – almost exclusively during the early years of its existence. Second, the pursuit of

Table 1.1 Categories of crime and numbers of accused dealt with by the Spanish Inquisition, 1540–1700

	Aragón		Castile		Total per crime	
	Number	%	Number	%	Number	%
Major Heresies						
Judaism	942	3.6	3,455	18.4	4,397	9.8
Islam	7,472	28.8	3,345	17.8	10,817	24.2
Lutheranism	2,284	8.8	1,219	6.5	3,503	7.8
Illuminism	61	0.2	82	0.4	143	0.3
Sub total	10,759	41.5	8,101	43.1	18,860	42.2
Minor Heresies						
Propositions	5,888	22.7	6,229	33.2	12,117	27.1
Bigamy	1,591	6.1	1,054	5.6	2,645	5.9
Solicitation	695	2.7	436	2.3	1,131	2.5
Acts against Inq.	2,139	8.3	1,232	6.6	3,371	7.5
Superstition	2,571	9.9	961	5.1	3,532	7.9
Miscellaneous	2,247	8.6	771	4.1	3,018	6.7
Sub total	15,131	58.4	10,683	56.9	25,814	57.7
Total trials	25,890	100	18,784	100	44,674	100
Death sentences						
In person	520	2.0	306	1.6	826	1.8
In effigy	291	1.1	487	2.6	778	1.7

Source: Contreras and Henningsen, 1986, p. 114

'Major Heresy' (as practised by *conversos, moriscos,* Illuminists and Lutherans) accounted for little more than 40 per cent or two-fifths of inquisitorial activity between 1540 and 1700 – the central period of the Inquisition's existence. Third, from 1540 the Holy Office was overwhelmingly concerned with the unorthodox behaviour of Old Christians accused of 'Minor Heresy', including outbursts against the faith (referred to as 'propositions'), blasphemy, unrestrained sexual behaviour, superstitious practices and opposition to the Holy Office. These lesser offences constituted three-fifths (just under 60 per cent) of inquisitorial business. The investigations of Henningsen and Contreras suggest that in the post-Tridentine period Spanish inquisitors were kept far busier by the misdemeanours of Old Christians than by those of dissident religious minorities. Having all but eliminated the incidence of Major Heresy, the primary function of the Holy Office during the 1560s and 1570s became that of prosecuting the sin of popular ignorance and of instructing Spaniards on matters of morality and the faith in accordance with the recommendations of the Council of Trent, a task it undertook with characteristic efficiency. Sixty-six per cent fewer cases of Minor Heresy came before the tribunals of the Inquisition after 1615. Finally, the data-bank study reveals that the activity of the Inquisition declined dramatically during the seventeenth century. Between 1560 and 1614 an average of 507 cases were examined per year; this figure fell to 168 cases per year between 1615 and 1700. By the late eighteenth century the Inquisition bore little resemblance to what it had been in 1480. Any judgement of the institution must therefore take into account the historical period and context in which it operated (Contreras and Henningsen, 1986, pp. 100–29).

The Four Seasons of the Inquisition

The most detailed set of trial statistics has come from Jean-Pierre Dedieu's exhaustive study of around 12,000 cases brought before the tribunal of Toledo, situated in the heart of Castile, over its entire existence between 1483 and 1820. On the basis of his research, Dedieu proposed that the activity of the Inquisition as a whole be divided into four distinct 'seasons' or chronological periods, according to prevailing religious, social and political conditions (Dedieu, 1979a, pp. 15–41; Contreras, 1997, pp. 35–52).

First period: 1480–1525

During the first 30 years of its life over half of all those tried by the Spanish Inquisition were brought before its tribunals. This was the period of maximum repression when victims were hounded out without mercy and punishments were applied with full rigour. The motivation for such extreme intolerance was the fear that newly converted Jews (*conversos*) might contaminate their Christian neighbours by their continued practice of Jewish rites and so threaten the authority and stability of the established Church. As baptized Christians, they were guilty of heresy against the faith. Toledo, Ciudad Real, Seville, Córdoba, Valencia and Barcelona were the main focal points of inquisitorial activity in these early years. The strategy was very similar in each urban location: inquisitors sought to break the internal cohesion of *converso* communities and to expose Jewish cells within families and neighbourhoods. On arriving in a town, inquisitors would meet with local officials and request their collaboration in calling people to a 'Sermon of the Faith', held in their church on Sunday after Mass. An edict was read out listing manifestations of Jewish heresy and inviting, in the first instance, self-confession and reconciliation to the Church within a defined 'period of grace'. But those who confessed their own guilt also became informants: their practice was linked to that of others.

It has been estimated that, at most, around 2,000 people died at the hands of the Inquisition in the period up to 1530, while perhaps as many as 15,000 were 'reconciled' – disciplined, but not sent to the stake. The Inquisition, although less brutal than we might have imagined, nevertheless generated an atmosphere of acute fear in Spanish society: fear of heresy on the one hand and fear of the consequences of being denounced on the other. Heresy, of course, was less real than imagined. It was a suitably explosive concept that, given the prevailing religious climate, was deliberately exaggerated to justify the institution's ends. Modern evidence suggests that what really lay behind the Jewish witch-hunt were deep-rooted social tensions and divisions that originated during the Christian Reconquest of Spain in the thirteenth and fourteenth centuries and that subsequently found their expression in the regime of religious and racial victimization pursued via the Holy Office. The practices of the Inquisition in its early years were arbitrary, including the acceptance of false witnesses who made unsubstantiated charges, the confiscation of goods and property and the indiscriminate use of torture. Its 'success' can be measured by the dramatic decrease in trials of Judaizers after 1520 and the subsequent reduction in the number of regional tribunals. We should not forget that only a relatively small proportion of the *converso* community came in contact with the Inquisition during the years of terror. The majority were well integrated into Christian society and accepted its values and traditions, so much so that they were barely recognizable as converts.

Second period: 1525–1630

This long period of over a century in the Inquisition's history has been the focus of much recent research. It was a period of relative stability in institutional terms: tribunals and procedural methods were both well established. In terms of its area of responsibility, this was fundamentally altered by the emergence of the Protestant Church in northern Europe and the potential threat this posed to the established Church. The Inquisition responded by widening its net of inquiry, firstly to encompass Protestant heresy (of negligible impact in Spain) and subsequently other forms of minor deviance from Catholic belief. In so doing, it considerably expanded its power base in Spanish society. The Catholic Church meanwhile engaged in its own process of reform, prompted by the proceedings of the Council of Trent, which as we have seen encompassed a renewal of the doctrines of faith and their moral and ethical application to the lives of orthodox Christians. While parish priests instructed their flocks, inquisitors undertook to ensure that the ideals of Trent were being carried through in practice and abuses corrected. What they encountered on their visitations were wide-ranging forms of conduct that revealed a misguided, widespread misunderstanding of what it meant to be a Catholic. In the second half of the sixteenth century, the work of the Inquisition became dominated by cases of minor heresy. Old Christians were brought before its tribunals for committing blasphemy, bigamy or sodomy, for ignorant outbursts about the faith, for superstitious beliefs and for loose moral behaviour. They received punishments appropriate to their offences: a public penance, a fine or service as a rower on the Spanish galleys. In the eyes of the Catholic hierarchy, the end justified the means: to extend the mission of the Church and enforce an absolute adherence to its structures of belief. There were physical limitations to the work of inquisitors in this field:

some rural areas were simply too difficult to reach and here, as a result, ignorance in matters of the faith persisted.

The Inquisition was not solely concerned with Protestants or Old Christians during this second phase of its activity. In the late 1560s, following the renewal of disturbances in the Alpujarras region of Granada and the advance of the Turk in the Mediterranean, it hardened its pursuit of *moriscos* (Moorish converts), suspected of committing religious offences. Forced to convert to Christianity at the beginning of the century, the *moriscos* lived in separate communities (concentrated in Granada in the south and Valencia in the east) where they preserved intact their native traditions and beliefs. All attempts to incorporate them into the Catholic Church failed. As a result they remained marginalized and their presence was increasingly resented by the civil and ecclesiastical authorities who were unable to deal with them effectively. The policy of repression culminated in the expulsion of the *moriscos* from Spain between 1609 and 1614.

Third period: 1630–1725

The Inquisition continued to play a vigilant role in the pursuit of minor heresy but a less prominent and vigorous one. Instead it was the crypto-Jew who once again fell victim to its procedures over this period. In 1492 a number of Spanish Jews settled in Portugal where they officially became *conversos* in their adopted land. For most of the first half of the sixteenth century they lived free from any form of religious or ethnic persecution. The Portuguese Inquisition, operative from 1547, allowed this situation to prevail in exchange for financial concessions. However, following the subjection of Portugal to Spanish rule in 1580, the Inquisition stepped up its activity against New Christians and dealt with them harshly. Over 200 were condemned to death in 50 *autos de fe* held in Lisbon, Evora and Coimbra between 1581 and 1600. This resulted in an influx of Portuguese New Christians into Castile, hoping for greater compassion from the Inquisition in Spain than they now found in their native land. They also brought with them highly sought-after skills in commerce and finance which they were able to trade for immunity from inquisitorial prosecution. At the beginning of the seventeenth century arguments were being voiced in senior religious and political circles in favour of adopting a more tolerant attitude towards the *converso* community, which helped to support their cause. A papal brief of August 1604 allowed for 400 Portuguese New Christians to be absolved from past offences and released on pardon from imprisonment in exchange for a payment of nearly 2 million ducats to Philip III. During the years following the pardon, many *cristaos-novos* flocked to the Spanish court to offer their financial services to the Crown. But when the terms of the pardon expired six years later and persecutions resumed, many Portuguese New Christians fled Spain.

Policy was reversed again in the mid-1620s. Under pressure from Philip IV, who was facing a serious financial crisis, the Holy Office granted Portuguese financiers suspected of crypto-Judaism a temporary reprieve from prosecution, facilitating their access to financial contracts and trading agreements throughout the Spanish Empire. By 1640 half of the loans that the Crown depended upon to service its debts were negotiated by Portuguese New Christian bankers. For traditionalists within the Church this was tantamount to the needs of a bankrupt exchequer being put before the preservation of orthodoxy. A plan put forward by the first minister Olivares to allow exiled Jews to return to Spain, first discussed in 1634, raised further serious concerns. When Portugal re-asserted its independence from the Spanish monarchy in 1640, the Inquisition responded by re-launching its attack on the minority of Portuguese New Christians left in Spain – now turned political opponents. Whole families were apprehended in Madrid. The tribunals of Toledo and Cuenca recorded dramatic increases in numbers of trials of crypto-Jews. The rigorous pursuit of Portuguese New Christians, which intensified during the 1650s, once again revived latent anti-semitic tensions in Spanish society. By the end of the seventeenth century, the first generation of Portuguese New Christians had effectively been wiped out but the Jewish convert, on account of his class and wealth more than his creed, was to remain the irreconcilable enemy until well into the following century.

Fourth period: 1725–1834

During the final phase of its existence, the Holy Office found itself in conflict with the philosophical and intellectual currents emanating from France that influenced the policy of the Bourbon monarchy in Spain. Philip V (1700–46) did not seek to abolish the Inquisition but rather to bring it under his direct control. However, attempts to limit the temporal and jurisdictional authority of the Inquisition were greeted with staunch resistance from conservative forces within society. During the first half of the eighteenth century, the Inquisition was effectively controlled by the Jesuits who firmly rejected ideas and beliefs associated with the French Enlightenment and its pursuit of 'reason' and 'progress'. But the Society was soon to fall from favour. In 1767 Charles III expelled the Jesuits from Spain and in the following year issued a royal edict urging inquisitors to concern themselves with matters of the faith while the Crown assumed control over censorship. The Inquisition was fast becoming a caricature of a bygone age when it acted as guardian of the ideologies of the Habsburg regime. Its privileged position in the sacred order of society was now considerably diminished, along with its sphere of activity. Only three to four cases per year came before the Toledan tribunal in the later eighteenth century compared with over 200 during the sixteenth century. Ninety per cent of trials now concerned moral rather than heretical offences. The Napoleonic invasions of 1808 hastened its permanent demise as a growing rift emerged between the philosophies of Church and State. The Inquisition's firm opposition to liberal thinking and social change generated by the French Revolution brought calls, outlined at the Cortes of Cádiz of 1810–13, for the suppression of its privileges and the abolition of its legal powers on the grounds that it was an unconstitutional organization. The anti-inquisitorial lobby included members of the clerical estate seeking to reclaim authority over what it deemed to be its functional areas. The Inquisition enjoyed a stay of execution under Ferdinand VII, restored to the throne in 1814, but its days were numbered. In 1830 a papal brief revoked its powers in matters of heresy. On

15 July 1834, after 356 years of existence, the Holy Office was formally abolished by royal decree.

Conclusion

On 12 January 2000, to mark the Catholic Church's Jubilee, Pope John Paul II issued a document entitled *Memory and Reconciliation* in which he asked for forgiveness for the errors of the Church over its 2,000-year history. These included the medieval crusades, the excesses of the Inquisition, the persecution of Jews and the abuses inherent in the conquest and evangelization of the New World. Two years earlier a symposium on the Inquisition was held in Rome, at which the papacy took full responsibility for its historical role in the extirpation of heresy. This public act of self-criticism and apology followed in the wake of some 25 years of revisionist research by historians of the Inquisition which has attempted to put aside the ideological polarization that characterized the writing of its history in the nineteenth and early twentieth centuries. As a result of their substantial efforts and innovative approaches (to which the author is heavily indebted), we are now able to review the role of the Spanish Inquisition from a much wider, dispassionate perspective. This book aims to separate out some of the myths from the realities surrounding one of the most notorious institutions in history via a broad synthesis of current, alongside traditional, trends in inquisitorial research.

2 The Inquisition as an Institution

The Spanish Inquisition exercised both a secular and a religious function. It was a court of law that owed allegiance to the Crown with supreme authority to root out heresy and restore obedience to the Church. It served to reinforce the political as well as the ideological interests of the Catholic State. In terms of its administrative organization, it was a self-supporting body. It had its own leader, the Inquisitor General; its own ministry, the Council of Inquisition; its own courts, the tribunals of the Inquisition; its own prisons, district commissioners and local agents. In terms of its procedures, it adhered to a strict set of rules, stringent by modern-day standards, within which inquisitors endeavoured to act justly. Its longevity as an institution could be attributed to the effectiveness of its organization and control mechanisms.

The Office of Inquisitor General

At the apex of the Inquisition's power structure stood the Inquisitor General, one of the most powerful functionaries in Spain next to the king. Although nominated by the Spanish Crown, Inquisitors General were formally appointed to office by means of a papal brief issued from Rome, in much the same way as Spanish bishops were elevated to office, for it was from the pope that the ecclesiastical authority of Inquisitors General ultimately derived. The majority of sixteenth- and seventeenth-century

Inquisitors General were of high aristocratic origins, educated at one of the elite university colleges of Salamanca or Valladolid, with previous experience of senior ecclesiastical and/or inquisitorial office. The post represented the pinnacle of their professional career achievement. Between 1483 and 1818 a total of 45 Inquisitors General were appointed to oversee the joint operations of the Holy Office in the Secretariats of Castile and Aragón. During the sixteenth and seventeenth centuries the office of Inquisitor General was frequently linked to service within the higher echelons of the Spanish Church and State. Between 1483 and 1707, 16 of the 28 incumbents of the office were serving archbishops or bishops: five of Toledo, four of Seville, three of Plasencia and two of Cuenca. Six held the office of President of the Council of Castile and four were royal confessors. (See appendix to this chapter.) The power wielded by the Inquisitor General varied considerably according to the prevailing religious and political climate, the character of the individual and the influence they held with the Crown. As well as selecting his own candidates through whom he directed the work of the Inquisition, the Spanish monarch could also be instrumental in their dismissal (subject to papal approval) if circumstances demanded it.

Fernando de Valdés gained the reputation for being one of the most ruthless and ambitious holders of the office of Inquisitor General (1547–66) in the whole history of the institution. Valdés rose through the ranks of ecclesiastical and secular office under Charles V to become Archbishop of Seville in 1546 and Inquisitor General in 1547. Faced with the possibility of being removed from court as a result of his refusal to contribute funds towards the war against heresy in northern Europe, he successfully 'stage managed' the discovery of Protestant cells in Seville and Valladolid in 1558, thus securing his leadership of the institution at a critical moment in its history. The following year he orchestrated the arrest and imprisonment of the Archbishop of Toledo, his personal enemy, on a charge of heresy. But he had exceeded the limits of his powers and was forced to retire to his archbishopric of Seville in 1566, not on the direct instruction of Philip II, but that of Pius V.

Valdés was replaced at the Holy office by Diego de Espinosa, a priest trained in law who rose dramatically from the office of

councillor of Inquisition (1564) to that of President of the Council of Castile (1565), before being nominated as Inquisitor General (1566). He worked tirelessly in both senior administrative
roles, effectively acting as the king's *alter ego* in matters of
Church and State. He fell from royal favour shortly before his
death in 1572, not on account of any official misconduct as in the
case of Valdés, but because Philip II felt he had become too sure
of his own power (Martínez-Millán, 1994, pp. 189–228). Inquisitors General often found themselves in a vulnerable position
when there was a change of monarch. Pedro de Portocarrero
was ousted from his leadership of the Holy Office by Philip III in
1599. Appointed during the last years of Philip II's reign, Portocarrero ingratiated himself by putting forward the name of an
alleged *converso* as a councillor of Inquisition, thereby under-
mining its reputation as a bastion of orthodoxy. His successor,
Fernando Niño de Guevara – another servant of the former
administration – also became embroiled in the same controversy
and was 'retired' to the Archbishopric of Seville in 1602
(Williams, 1990, pp. 253–64).

   In the course of the first half of the seventeenth century, two
Dominicans were removed as Inquisitors General for furthering
their own interests and ambitions in office. From being a figure
of relative obscurity (the son of a cloth seller from Zaragoza),
Luis de Aliaga built up a power base at the court of Philip III via
his coveted confessorial relationship with the king (1608) and his
supernumerary role on the Council of Inquisition (1614). In
1618, in alliance with other senior figures at court, he successfully
mounted a challenge to the rule (*privanza*) of the Duke of Lerma.
The favourite's departure from court was swiftly followed by
Aliaga's appointment as Inquisitor General. But the Dominican's period of tenure was to be short-lived. As soon as Philip
IV succeeded to the throne in 1621 he obtained papal approval to
withdraw Aliaga's delegated powers on the grounds of his un-
worthiness. Antonio de Sotomayor also worked his way into
court circles as confessor to the king, a post he held for a total
of 30 years. He had previously been employed by the Inquisition
as both a *consultor* (theological adviser) and a *calificador* (censor)
and in 1622 took up the councillorship vacated by Aliaga. He also
served on the Councils of State and War (1624) and regularly

advised the monarch on matters of ecclesiastical policy. When he rose to become Inquisitor General in 1632, Sotomayor assumed the full reins of power placed at his disposal, freely engaging in the nepotistic distribution of inquisitorial and episcopal office. His corrupt exercise of patronage went unchecked for over a decade until the departure of the Count-Duke Olivares from court in 1643. Deprived of the support of the favourite, Soto-mayor was invited by the papacy to retire from the Holy Office on the grounds of his 'infirmities and incapacities'.

The last Inquisitor General to be forced out of office was Baltasar de Mendoza y Sandoval, bishop of Segovia. In 1700, in alliance with the queen consort, he accused the Dominican confessor Friolán Díaz (also a supernumerary member of the Council of Inquisition) of being complicit in the bewitching of Charles II. When other members of the Council found there was no case to answer, Mendoza appealed to Rome. This act of defiance proved to be his undoing and, following the interven-tion of Philip V, he left the Holy Office in disgrace in 1705 (Lea, 1922, I, pp. 305–14). Thereafter, as the work of the Inquisition became largely reduced to administrative routine, those appointed to the office of Inquisitor General tended to be non-controversial, non-political figures, over whom members of the Council of Inquisition increasingly held sway.

The Council of Inquisition

The Council of the Supreme and General Inquisition (known as the *Suprema*), presided over by the Inquisitor General, was first established in 1483, to co-ordinate the Inquisition's activities at local level in both Castile and Aragón. Its statutory membership fluctuated between five and six. Two councillors of Castile also regularly attended its sessions as well as the king's Dominican confessor from 1614. The *Suprema* met on Monday, Wednesday and Friday mornings and Tuesday, Thursday and Saturday afternoons. Although the Council of Inquisition was set up by Dominicans, it was not exclusively controlled or staffed by them, or by members of the secular clergy. From the middle of the sixteenth century, following structural reforms introduced by

Inquisitor General Valdés, a typical councillor of Inquisition was a native of Castile, of Old Christian ancestry, a member of the middle nobility, university-educated in law, with prior experience of service either as an inquisitor on one of the more prestigious local tribunals (such as Toledo, Seville, Córdoba, Granada or Valladolid) or within the state bureaucracy. It was common for a long-serving councillor of Inquisition to further his career as a bishop and/or use it as a springboard for promotion within government (Barrio Gozalo, 1999, pp. 109–14). Under Inquisitor General Aliaga (1619–22), nepotism began to feature in recruitment to the Council. At the same time, a power struggle emerged within the Holy Office with councillors seeking to extend their authority in making policy decisions over that of the Inquisitor General. The *Suprema* was fast developing into an enclosed oligarchy within the monarchy, made up of career professionals, hereditary office holders, as well as the royal confessor whose power was increasingly circumscribed by the infiltration of Jesuits into office. The attempts made by Philip IV to reform membership of the Council were met with loud opposition. The *Suprema* retained its key role within government by extending its areas of jurisdiction and imposing its own indispensability on the Crown (Martínez-Millán and Sánchez Rivilla, 1984, pp. 71–106).

The Council had a number of responsibilities. As well as acting as judge in all cases brought to appeal, it drew up instructions, known as *cartas acordadas*, according to which provincial tribunals were to conduct their business, sometimes modifying them to take account of political or religious circumstances. Under Inquisitor General Diego de Espinosa (1566–72) controls were tightened over the routine operations of regional tribunals which became subject to periodical inspections by visiting inquisitors to ensure that officials were not exceeding the boundaries of inquisitorial authority. From mid-century, annual reports (*relaciones de causas*) had to be submitted to Madrid, detailing cases concluded and *autos de fe* held. Local tribunals could be asked to explain their decisions and punishments might be reduced or increased accordingly. Under Espinosa's successor, Gaspar de Quiroga (1573–94), local autonomy was further eroded. Every death sentence now had to be approved by the *Suprema*. Early in the reign of Philip IV this ruling was extended

to all sentences involving perpetual imprisonment or severe physical punishment, such as galley service or whippings. It also
arbitrated in cases of discord and those that involved inquisitorial employees. This policy of centralization ensured that effectively from 1625 local tribunals could only deal with the most
trivial cases without being obliged to refer them to Madrid.
Furthermore, from 1632 each tribunal was required to submit a
monthly report (in place of the annual one) on all its current
cases to the *Suprema* for close scrutiny. Thus while the work of
the Inquisition in combating heresy was declining, the bureaucratic functions of the Council were increasing, along with the
number of secretarial staff it employed to carry out its work. The
related salary costs of the Council more than doubled from just
over 3,252,000 *maravedis* in 1568 to 7,000,000 in 1606, rising to
8,100,000 in 1625 (Martínez-Millán, 1993, pp. 919–20). By the
mid-seventeenth century and through to its extinction, it was
effectively managing all inquisitorial business despatched to it
by local tribunals to become the central organ of the Inquisition's administrative operations, considerably reducing the role
of the regional institutions (Lea, 1922, II, pp. 179–87; Monter,
1990, pp. 68–72).

The Inquisition in the Provinces

Provincial tribunals of the Inquisition were set up throughout
Spain (12 in Castile; four in Aragón, three in the Indies and two
pertaining to the Italian possessions) – the majority within the
first decade of the Inquisition's establishment – directly subject
to the *Suprema* in Madrid (see table 2.1). The regional tribunals
of the Inquisition were staffed by two or three inquisitors,
appointed on the basis of their academic background and em-
ployment record, as well as the purity of their ancestral origins.
They were predominantly of Castilian origin, graduates in law
rather than theology, seldom natives of the area where they
worked. Some had previously held other, lesser inquisitorial
offices or been employed within the Church. Local inquisitors
tended to serve for on average five years before moving up
the career ladder to a higher office within the Church–State

Table 2.1   Provincial Tribunals of the Spanish Inquisition

Secretariat of Castile	Tribunal established	Secretariat of Aragón	Tribunal established
Seville	1482	Zaragoza	1482
Córdoba	1482	Valencia	1482
Toledo	1485	Barcelona	1484
Llerena	1485	Mallorca	1488
Valladolid	1488		
Murcia	1488		
Cuenca	1489	Sicily	1487
Las Palmas	1507	Sardinia	1492
Logroño	1512	Lima	1570
Granada	1526	México	1571
Santiago	1574	Cartagena de Indias	1610
Madrid	1640		

Sources: Lea, 1922, I, pp. 541–5; Contreras and Dedieu, 1980, pp. 37–93.

bureaucracy. The tribunal of Toledo was one of the most prestigious in Castile. Of the 57 Toledan inquisitors who served between 1482 and 1598, 55 were graduates in law from one of the distinguished *colegios mayores*. Some simultaneously held cathedral canonries that financed their positions. Many went on to further their careers in senior governmental posts as well as within the higher echelons of ecclesiastical office. Of the aforementioned 57 Toledan inquisitors, 14 became members of the *Suprema*. Ten were promoted to bishoprics. Two rose to the office of Inquisitor General. Others went on to serve in the High Courts (*Chancillerías*) and as presidents of other major councils (Bennassar, 1979, pp. 84–5).

Provincial inquisitors were aided by three or four notaries (*notarios*), an assessor (*asesor*), a constable (*alguacil*) and a prosecutor (*fiscal*). With such a limited personnel, each tribunal relied heavily on the assistance of a number of local agents. Chief among them were district commissioners (*comisarios*) – for the most part parish priests – who effectively acted as inquisitors in remote areas. The commissioner received information, interrogated witnesses, made arrests, and in addition carried out a number of regular inspections. He was responsible for taking and sending denunciations to the tribunal and collecting evidence at the inquisitors' request for prosecutions to proceed. The network of *comisarios*, which expanded dramatically in the second half of the sixteenth century in response to the Counter-Reformation offensive, increased the Inquisition's effectiveness at local level. It removed the necessity for lengthy and costly visitations of districts by inquisitors themselves (Lea, 1922, II, pp. 268–72; Nalle, 1987a, pp. 566–7).

Each commissioner was assisted by lay agents, known as familiars (*familiares*), who principally acted as intermediaries between the tribunal and the prisoner. Contrary to popular belief, the role of the *familiar* was not to denounce crimes of heresy but to carry out investigations and collect testimony that might lead to denunciation. He always acted in conjunction with a notary and never independently. In Aragón the office of *familiar* attracted members of the professional classes (including clergy) while in the kingdom of Castile positions became entrenched within distinguished aristocratic families. There were between 10,000 and 12,000 *familiares* in Spain at the end of the sixteenth century. This figure increased during the early seventeenth century and then fell thereafter. In practice, the density and distribution of *familiares* varied enormously between regions and within them between town and countryside. In the kingdom of Valencia, a census of 1567 revealed that there were 1,638 *familiares*, or one per 42 households. Over half were to be found in the sparsely populated countryside in small settlements of less than 1,000 people where other forms of social control were at their weakest. The number of Valencian *familiares* fell to one per 64 households in 1602, their concentration shifting from rural to urban areas. This situation compared favourably to rural Galicia where only 226 villages (6.4 per cent of populated areas) had *familiares* in 1611, falling to 108 in 1641. The fact that significant parts of the peninsula, such as north-west Spain, never came in touch with inquisitorial officials meant that the impact of the institution was much more marginal than its critics have suggested (Contreras, 1987b, pp. 133–58; García-Cárcel and Moreno Martínez, 2000, pp. 135–42). The work of local agents was unpaid but their posts were highly sought after because of the prestige and privileges they carried with them. The most important of these rendered the office holder (whatever his status) untouchable by the secular authorities. In a civil or criminal case, he was subject to the jurisdiction of the Inquisition and was virtually guaranteed immunity from prosecution. Agents of the Inquisition were also exempt from paying certain taxes and occupied preferential positions in state ceremonies.

Inquisitors had been required since 1500 to carry out regular inspections of their districts (known as *visitas de distrito*) in search of malefactors. In each town or village they visited, they were to read the edict of faith and take testimonies from those who came forward with information about religious deviance. Lesser offenders received an instant admonishment but more serious ones had to be referred back to the tribunal. In some remote areas visitations were of crucial importance in the denunciation process. A ten-month visitation of the entire Basque country that took place between 1538 and 1539 resulted in nearly 200 accusations being made, a quarter of them for witchcraft. In 1570 new regulations were issued concerning *visitas*. Henceforth, every tribunal was obliged to send one of its three inquisitors on a visitation through some part of its district for at least four months of every year and produce a progress report. Failure to comply resulted in the inquisitor responsible losing one third of his annual salary. Visitations took up to half of an inquisitor's time for very little return, leaving urgent cases pending in the district's headquarters. In some remote rural areas, villagers responded to these inspections by erecting a barrier of silence. The Toledan tribunal held thirty-four *visitas* from 1540 to 1579, covering its entire district several times, but only half as many during the following 40 years. From 1580 the number of denunciations prompted via visitations declined dramatically (Dedieu, 1977, pp. 235–56) (see table 2.2). The official requirement was reduced under Philip III to a one-third territorial inspection every year. After 1620, inquisitors in Castile and Aragón regularly sought exemption from making *visitas* and their requests were duly granted. As a result they virtually ceased from this juncture. Local tribunals became more sedentary, preoccupied with bureaucratic procedures rather than actively seeking out delinquents (Monter, 1990, pp. 66–8).

Table 2.2   Outcomes of a sample of visitations made by Inquisitors of Toledo, 1556–1607

Number of cases	1556	1566	1571	1573	1574	1578	1583	1607
Leading to instant condemnation	139	25	15	28	23	—	—	—
Deferred to local tribunal	10	5	10	37	6	?	?	?
For which information gathered	—	many	81	137	77	72	59	24
Totals	149	30++	106	202	106	72	59	24

Source: Dedieu, 1977, p. 247

The Procedures of the Inquisition

The Spanish Inquisition functioned according to a set of clearly defined rules, modified over time. The *Instrucciones* of the first Inquisitor General, Tomás de Torquemada, in 1485 provided a summary of the philosophy and methods of the Inquisition in Spain and was to become the established handbook for the work of local tribunals. In the light of the experiences of the first 80 years of the Inquisition's activity, which included regional variations of practice, a revised set of guidelines was produced by the Inquisitor General Fernando de Valdés in 1561 (although not issued for general use until the mid-seventeenth century). The new instructions detailed all the various procedures to be followed in an inquisition hearing, from the first detection of heresy through to the allocation of punishment, and are thus a valuable source of information for the historian (Jiménez Monteserín, 1980, pp. 198–240).

When inquisitors arrived in a district, they arranged for the reading of an 'edict of faith' after Mass on a designated Sunday at which all local residents would be in attendance. At the end of the sermon everyone was obliged to swear a solemn oath of allegiance to the Holy Inquisition. The local inquisitor then read aloud the edict, comprising a long list of heresies against the Catholic faith (Jewish, Islamic, Illuminist, Lutheran etc.). This was followed by an invitation to all those present to acknowledge their own sins as well as to denounce their friends and neighbours for engaging in such offences. (During its early years the Inquisition permitted those who confessed during an initial 30- to 40-day period of grace to be reconciled to the Church without penalty.) The congregation was under moral obligation to comply with the inquisitor's wishes. Denunciations to the Inquisition were commonly based on long-standing disputes between members of the local community rather than on verifiable evidence of heresy. The fear of being exposed to public scrutiny by their neighbours (rather than fear of the Inquisition *per se*) prompted many false confessions of guilt. The collaboration of ordinary people was thus fundamental to the Inquisition's work on the ground and particularly so in areas where social discord was rife (Kamen, 1997, pp. 174–9).

Not every denunciation automatically led to arrest and sentencing. It marked the preliminary stage in the identification of a heretic. Before deciding whether to take the case further, inquisitors summoned theological assessors or advisers, known as *calificadores*, to determine whether the offence fell within a designated category of heresy. If there was sufficient evidence to support a hearing, the prosecutor (*fiscal*) could then order the arrest of the suspect. This was the responsibility of the *alguacil* (the arresting officer) who at the same time confiscated all the goods of the accused, taking as many of their assets as was necessary to support their needs while in prison, as well as those of any dependants. After the arrest, the accused was taken away to solitary confinement within the secret prisons of the Inquisition to await their trial. Contrary to popular conception, conditions in inquisitorial prisons were generally a lot better than in those that served the needs of the civil and ecclesiastical authorities. As a result some prisoners attempted various strategies, including making blasphemous remarks and pretending they were Protestants, in order to get themselves transferred from secular prisons to those belonging to the Inquisition. If a prisoner fell ill he was allowed access to a doctor as well as a confessor if he so desired. He was fed a diet of seasonal foods and if wealthy enough he could choose his own menu. Inquisitors were required to inspect their prisons several times per year to ensure that these standards were being adhered to.

The case against the accused began with a series of three separate hearings. The aim of these preliminary sessions was to arouse the prisoner's sense of guilt, to force him to confess his heresy and repent. At the first stage of questioning he was required to provide personal details about his upbringing, his education and travels abroad. He was asked whether he knew the reason for his arrest and was advised to examine his conscience carefully. The inquisitors tried to judge the soul of the accused, to discover whether or not his deeds reflected a system of belief that deviated from that of the established church. They endeavoured, at least when dealing with Old Christians, to lead them back to orthodox ways. If after three such sessions (lasting up to three weeks), no confession was forthcoming, the prosecutor of the tribunal made the formal charge in the presence of the accused and inquisitors, with details of the category of heresy involved. The accused was immediately required to answer the individual points of the charge. He did so under oath to tell the truth at all times, with no allowance for reflection or reference to the written indictment. All his statements were noted down, including negative responses to questions. Following this initial interrogation, the accused was allowed the services of a lawyer (*abogado de preso*) with whom he could consult in the presence of an inquisitor. The duty of the lawyer – appointed by the Inquisition and not the accused – was not so much to defend his client but to make sure that he complied with all the tribunal's requirements and ultimately to persuade him to admit his guilt, beg for mercy and seek re-admittance to the Church.

The case now proceeded to a trial (*prueba*). Witnesses were re-called and their statements verified and put together in the standard format: 'In this month of this year *a certain person* stated that at such a place and such a time he saw the accused say this or that.' The accused was given a copy of the evidence brought against him (with the names of witnesses removed) and was required to give an immediate response to the charges. He then had various options. He could call upon favourable witnesses who would support his reputation as a good Christian. He could disable hostile ones (by proving personal enmity or demonstrating that they were untrustworthy people) or call upon 'extenuating circumstances' to explain his behaviour, such as drunkenness or insanity. It was left to the discretion of inquisitors whether to investigate matters further. At the end of the day it was often a question of the word of the defendant against that of others whose identity remained unknown. Although not all victims were accused and sentenced on the grounds of false evidence or forced confessions, it is true that inquisitors, in their zeal to save souls, tended to make statements made by the accused fit in with the denunciation of witnesses rather than examining all the facts (Henningsen, 1980, p. 43).

Torture was one of the tools that the Spanish Inquisition, in common with other ecclesiastical and secular tribunals, had at its disposal to extract a confession from a defendant. But it was employed far less frequently and less severely than popular myth suggests. Most prisoners either confessed without torture or were convicted on the basis of multiple testimony. The results of modern research suggest that around a quarter of those charged with major heresy were subject to torture and a much lower ratio (under 5 per cent) of those charged with minor offences. It was applied selectively at certain periods, notably against Judaizers in the later seventeenth century, rather than consistently throughout. The three main forms of torture used by the Inquisition were the rack (*potro*), which involved the victim being held on a rack by cords pulled ever more tightly around the limbs until he confessed; the pulley (*garrucha*), whereby the accused was weighted by his feet and raised to the ceiling before being jerked back to the ground; and the *toca*, which involved the enforced consumption of jars of water. Clearly these procedures, when applied with full rigour, left prisoners scarred and humiliated but they were more regularly practised in moderation to induce a confession, at which point the torture ceased. Confessions made under torture, which had to be verified by the prisoner 24 hours later, were contributory but not necessarily decisive factors in the final judgement of a case. Inquisitors themselves were sceptical of the efficacy and validity of torture as a method of conviction. From 1625, all cases involving torture had to be referred for judgement to the *Suprema* in Madrid. As a result local tribunals resorted to it less frequently (Monter, 1990, pp. 74–5; Kamen, 1997, pp. 188–92).

When all the documentary evidence had been gathered, a 'jury' or *consulta de fe*, consisting of the tribunal's inquisitors, a representative of the local bishop (*el ordinario*) and several legal or theological advisers (*consultores*), could proceed to a vote on the guilt of the accused and on the sentence to be imposed, although this was not officially announced until the *auto de fe*. If there were differences of opinion among inquisitors, these were to be submitted to the *Suprema*. There were four possible outcomes: the accused was either (a) acquitted, (b) penanced, (c) reconciled, or (d) sentenced to death either in person or in effigy (also referred to as being relaxed to the secular arm). An acquittal meant that the case was absolved or suspended due to insufficient or inconclusive evidence, although the accused remained under suspicion. To be penanced was the least punishment to be inflicted and usually applied to those who confessed their guilt. Penances, accompanied by 'abjurations' of errors, were allocated according to the gravity of the offence committed. For a lesser offence such as bigamy or blasphemy a light penance was imposed (*de levi*) and a heavier one (*de vehementi*) for more serious offences. Those penanced for light offences – confined for the period of their penance to a house of correction (*casa de penitencia*) – received a pardon and were admitted back into the Church, but were stripped of their assets and had to wear the penitential garment (*sanbenito*) for a fixed period of time. The garment – a tunic made of yellow linen or cloth – bore one or two red diagonal crosses on the reverse, accompanied by flames and dragons for more grave offences. The *sanbenito* was subsequently put on display in the parish church to which the condemned man or woman officially belonged with their name attached and was replaced when it showed signs of wear and tear. It thus acted as a constant humiliating reminder of the memory of their sin and a warning to the faithful not to veer from the course of orthodoxy. Although theoretically pardoned, he or she remained permanently outcast by society and their infamy extended throughout their family over several generations. They were not permitted to compete for certain jobs or professions, to carry arms or to distinguish themselves via the wearing of expensive clothes or jewellery. Those who abjured *de vehementi* and then later relapsed were 'reconciled'. This meant that they became subject to much more severe punishments, including flogging, galley service, seizure of goods, a punitive prison sentence and the indefinite wearing of the *sanbenito*. If found guilty subsequently, a reconciled heretic would be treated as a relapsed one and handed over to the secular authorities for yet harsher punishment. (Around 80 per cent of all victims of the Inquisition were either penanced or reconciled.) The severest penalty to be allotted was to be burnt at the stake at a site outside the city following the *auto de fe*. Two and a quarter per cent of all victims of the Inquisition (637 individuals) were condemned to death in person between 1560 and 1614. This figure fell to one per cent (142 individuals) between 1615 and 1700. Over the full time span, a further 1.4 per cent (750 individuals) went to the flames in effigy, having already died or escaped justice (Contreras and Henningsen, 1986, pp.117–19). If neither the acquittal nor the conviction of a prisoner was possible on account of unsatisfactory evidence, he or she was to recant and pay a fine. In this way the Inquisition retained its authority and the accused remained 'suspect' for the rest of his or her life (Lea, 1922, III, pp. 121–81).

Every aspect of the Inquisition's activity was shrouded in secrecy, giving rise to the popular saying: *Con el rey y la inquisición, chitón!* (Keep silence as far as the king and the Inquisition are concerned!) This rule of silence applied to all its employees, from its own officials down to its consultants and lay agents, as well as its witnesses who faced being excommunicated and fined if they made known their testimony. The names of informers were recorded in books kept for each tribunal (*los libros de los testificados*). Not only were denunciations secret, so were trial records, accessible only to inquisitors and their officials. The Inquisition was under no obligation to account for those it held in its own prisons. They simply disappeared from public view for the duration of their trial, reappearing once their sentence was passed a year or two later. Upon his or her release, the accused was sworn not to reveal anything about his case or that of other prisoners he came in contact with. Very rarely was this wall of secrecy breached. Inquisitors believed that secrecy and justice were interconnected: that their freedom from outside intervention enabled them to make unbiased investigations. Secrecy precluded bribery and was seen to guarantee fairness. However, from the public perspective, as well as that of the prisoner, ignorance of its workings gave rise to fears of injustice and led to a questioning of the validity of its authority (Monter, 1990, pp. 72–3; Henningsen, 1980, p. 39).

When judged alongside twenty-first-century legal practice, the procedures of the Inquisition fall a long way short of the norms of acceptability. To make the outcome of a case rest on the ability of the accused person to prove his or her innocence would today be inadmissible. However, from the evidence at our disposal, it is clear that in general inquisitors endeavoured to act fairly within their own framework of justice. False witnesses were severely reprimanded and anyone wrongly accused had the right to appear at an *auto de fe* carrying a palm branch as a symbol of their vindication before the Holy Office. A concern for justice (and the wish to avoid making erroneous accusations) could have been a reason why trials lasted so long. There were also deliberate delays built into the system which served to bring the fullest weight of evidence against the accused. On average most inquisitorial tribunals heard no more than 50 cases per year (one per week). When judging the Spanish Inquisition, we must recall that the Spanish secular courts had an extremely poor reputation for the quality of justice they delivered, while the ecclesiastical courts were renowned for the leniency of their judgements (Henningsen, 1980, p. 45).

SUMMARY OF INQUISITORIAL TRIAL PROCEDURE

1   Denunciation
2   Decision to institute proceedings
3   Collection of evidence
4   Qualification of crime
5   Decision to prosecute
6   Arrest
7   Interrogation of accused
8   Formal accusation
9   Summary of charges communicated to accused
10   Vote on the sentence
11   Sentencing
12   *Auto de fe*

Source: Dedieu, 1987, p. 133

The *Auto de Fe*

Once the severity of the crime had been decided upon, the inquisitors had to fix a date for the formal announcement of the penalty
via an *auto de fe*. There were two types of ceremony: an *auto
público general* or an *auto particular* (also known as an *autillo*).
The former was a grandiose occasion held in the *plaza mayor* or
main town square to which all civic and ecclesiastical dignitaries
were invited. It usually coincided with a public holiday and
attracted huge crowds. Sentences were read during the day and
those condemned to death executed before nightfall. *Autillos*, by
contrast, were semi-private (and less costly) affairs, often held in a
church before a small audience, usually for minor offences and
involving less public humiliation. Between 1575 and 1610 the
tribunal of Toledo held 12 *autos públicos* at which 386 culprits
appeared, while 786 cases were settled in *autos particulares*. This
trend away from the celebration of public *autos* continued into the
seventeenth century (Lea, 1922, III, pp. 220–1).

   The public *auto de fe* was a meticulously planned, stage-
managed theatrical event. The cost and preparation involved
meant that they were held only infrequently. Dates were chosen
to coincide with special religious feasts, often those associated
with the triumph of the cross. Once the *Suprema* had approved the
staging of the *auto*, its elaborate organization began. Special
invitations went out to the participating authorities whose presence was vital to the outcome of the event. Inquisitorial officials
(*familiares*), as well as notaries and town criers, went around the
locality, carrying the banner of the Inquisition (a green cross
flanked on one side by an olive branch of mercy and on the
other by a sword of justice) and blowing loud trumpets inviting
people to attend the *auto* on the stipulated date. There were also
material preparations: the penitential robes and hats worn by the
accused had to be made, as well as the green crosses carried by
members of the inquisitorial procession. In addition, two large
raised stages had to be built on the site in the main square of the
town – one for the penitents on trial and one for inquisitorial,
ecclesiastical, municipal and royal officials, for whom attendance
was compulsory. The windows and balconies of houses

overlooking the town square were reserved for important dignitaries. As well as fulfilling a didactic purpose, the *auto* also served
as a carefully choreographed illustration of order and rank in
society, dominated by elite members of the religious and political
communities.

AN ACCOUNT OF THE *AUTO DE FE* HELD IN TOLEDO ON SUNDAY 12
FEBRUARY, 1486

All the reconciled went in procession, to the number of 750 persons,
including both men and women. They went in procession from the
church of St Peter Martyr in the following way. The men were all
together in a group, bareheaded and unshod, and since it was extremely cold they were told to wear soles under their feet which were
otherwise bare; in their hands were unlit candles. The women were
together in a group, their heads uncovered and their faces bare, unshod
like the men and with candles. Among all these were many prominent
men in high office. With the bitter cold and the dishonour and disgrace
they suffered from the great number of spectators (since a great many
people from outlying districts had come to see them), they went along
howling loudly and weeping and tearing out their hair, no doubt more
for the dishonour they were suffering than for any offence they had
committed against God. Thus they went in tribulation through the
streets along which the Corpus Christi procession goes, until they came
to the cathedral. At the door of the church were two chaplains who
made the sign of the cross on each one's forehead, saying, 'Receive the
sign of the cross, which you denied and lost through being deceived.'
Then they went into the church until they arrived at a scaffolding
erected by the new gate, and on it were the father inquisitors. Nearby
was another scaffolding on which stood an altar at which they said
mass and delivered a sermon. After this a notary stood up and began to
call each one by name, saying, 'Is x here?' The penitent raised his
candle and said, 'Yes.' There in public they read all the things in
which he had judaized. The same was done for the women. When
this was over they were publicly allotted penance and ordered to go
in procession for six Fridays, disciplining their body with scourges of
hempcord, barebacked, unshod and bareheaded; and they were to fast
for those six Fridays. It was also ordered that all the days of their life
they were to hold no public office such as *alcalde, alguacil, regidor* or
jurado, or to be public scriveners or messengers, and that those who
held these offices were to lose them. And that they were not to become
moneychangers, shopkeepers, or grocers or hold any official post
whatsoever. And they were not to wear silk or scarlet or coloured

cloths or gold or silver or pearls or coral or any jewels. Nor could they stand as witnesses. And they were ordered that if they relapsed, that is if they fell into the same error again, and resorted to any of the fore mentioned things, they would be condemned to the fire. And when all this was over they went away at two o'clock in the afternoon.

Source: Kamen, 1997, pp. 207–8

The day of the *auto* began with the celebration of Mass in the local parish church adjacent to the square where the ceremony would take place. From early morning onwards the accused were led along the processional route accompanied by *familiares*. Those guilty of lesser crimes (and therefore liable for lesser punishment) appeared first, while those who refused repentance, and therefore faced execution, marched last. As the penitents walked along the streets, filled with excited crowds, they were greeted with an outpouring of emotions in the form of jeers, shouts and gestures. The *auto* lasted well into the night, an exhausting, cathartic form of psychological theatre, charged with symbolic meaning. It reached its climax with the reading aloud of the crimes each prisoner was accused of and the delivery of their sentence. This was the first opportunity that the general public had of knowing why their friend or neighbour had disappeared from the community (Thomas, 2001, p. 96). Some of those accused were reconciled to the Church but always with a penalty to pay, such as a physical beating, a public penance, a fine or the confiscation of goods. Others (recalcitrant and relapsed heretics) were taken away on the backs of donkeys by the civil authorities to the *quemadero* (the site for burnings, on the outskirts of the city) to meet their death that same evening.

The function of the ceremonial *auto de fe* was essentially pedagogical: to publicly proclaim the supremacy of the Catholic faith by cleansing the Church of its most abhorrent enemies. It was both a theatre for the condemnation of those accused of heresy as well as an occasion for a public sermon (the *Sermón de la Fe*) addressed to an audience of thousands of spectators. In this way the *auto* resembled a communal 'act of faith' in which sinners and believers took part. By witnessing the sentencing of those who contravened the code of orthodoxy, the public reaffirmed their rejection of those who did not conform to the Old Christian model and their acceptance of the dominant order. The *auto de fe* equally sought to strike at the conscience of those who marched to meet their fate. The repentance, submission (and reconciliation in most cases) of those indicted was an essential part of the spectacle. The *auto de fe* was a part-religious, part-judicial ceremony that taught a lesson to all those present, the faithful and the non-faithful, of what the consequences of non-submission might be before the tribunal of faith on earth and its counterpart, the divine court on high. Behind the pomp, ceremony and entertainment the purpose of the *auto de fe*, in imitation of the Inquisition itself, was to instil salutary fear. Non-participation in the celebration of Catholic hegemony implied non-conformity and withdrawal from the community of believers – a potentially offensive form of behaviour that might lead to inquisitorial investigation, social exclusion and ultimate damnation (Alpert, 2001, pp. 130–8; Avilés, 1987, pp. 249–64; Flynn, 1991, pp. 281–97; González de Caldas, 1987, pp. 266–72; Ruiz, 2001, pp. 155–60).

AN ACCOUNT OF THE *AUTO DE FE* HELD IN THE PLAZA MAYOR OF MADRID OF 4 JULY 1632

On June 20, 1632 ... Madrid began to stir with intensive preparations for one of the greatest *autos de fe* ever to be held in the city. On that day, in accordance with established procedure, public notices were posted which announced that the *auto* would be held two weeks later. The standard of the Inquisition was carried through the streets, and a proclamation was read to the populace. In the following days the Plaza Mayor resounded with noise of hammers and saws as workmen constructed the necessary platforms and scaffolding. Care was taken to place the seats for the king and queen in those balconies which would afford them both shade and unobstructed vision. [...] The prisoners were secretly transferred one night from Toledo, where they had been held until now, to the new prisons of the Inquisition in Madrid. The work in the Plaza Mayor was completed with a final touch when awnings were stretched over the balconies and platforms reserved for royalty and nobility. [...]

On Saturday July 3rd at 5.00 p.m., the Procession of the Green Cross (*Cruz Verde*) emerged from the Colegio de Doña María de Aragón. It was preceded by the standard of the Holy Office, displaying the arms of the Holy Office (*Misericordia y Justicia*) on one side, and the arms of the king on the other, carried aloft by Don Alonso Enríquez de Cabrera, who was a familiar of the Inquisition. Next came the banners of the *Cruz Blanca* and the *Cruz Verde*. The procession wound its way to the royal palace and thence to the Plaza Mayor, where the *Cruz Verde* was placed at a specially constructed altar, and a guard stationed around it for the night.

Before dawn on July 4, the day of the *auto*, masses began to be celebrated at the altar, with a large crowd of people already in attendance. The various platforms began to be decorated with damasks of various colours and when dawn broke another mass was sung by the Dominicans. [...] By now the great square was almost filled. The councils of Castile, Aragón, Italy, Portugal, Flanders and the Indies were seated. At 7.00 a.m. Their Majesties and the Infante Don Carlos left the palace in a coach, together with Olivares and other grandees, their wives, and attendants. Entering the Plaza Mayor through the houses of the Count of Barajas, they too took their places. Meanwhile the procession of the accused had left the prisons of the Inquisition. As they made their way toward the square, along the route there was such a number of people gathered for the occasion at the windows, doors, roofs and scaffolds, that the imagination could not encompass it.

The prisoners were finally marched into the Plaza Mayor, followed by the officials and dignitaries of the Holy Office and of the city of Madrid. The very last to enter was Cardinal Antonio Zapata, Inquisitor-General of the kingdoms of Spain. Ascending to the royal balcony, he administered to Philip the oath that he would continue to defend the Faith and give all possible support to the Holy Office. With this ceremony the *auto*, which was to last until the evening, was officially begun. A sermon was preached by Fray Antonio de Sotomayor, at this time confessor to the king, but himself soon to become the Grand Inquisitor. After the judges were sworn in, each of the prisoners appeared holding a yellow candle and wearing the peaked paper hat (*coraza*) on his head. Those who were to be relaxed for burning held a green cross in their hands. In all, 40 prisoners appeared in person. Twenty-four received penances for crimes other than judaising, while nine were penanced for it. But of the seven who were sentenced to be burned at the stake, the proportion was reversed. Six of them were condemned Judaisers, and only one was not: a Genoese friar who had been convicted of heresy and sacrilege. Finally, four Judaisers (two of them already dead, and the other having fled the country) were sentenced to be burned in effigy. [...]

The *auto* came to an end at 6.00 p.m. The Plaza Mayor was emptied, the penanced were returned to their cells, and the Dominicans took the *Cruz Verde* to the Monastery of St Thomas. [...] Later in the evening, the condemned were brought to the *brasero*, the place of execution which had been built for the occasion outside the Puerta de Alcalá.

Source: Yerushalmi, 1971, pp. 105–10 (based on anonymous *Relación* of 1632)

The Finances of the Inquisition

One of the many criticisms levelled against the Inquisition was that it profited from the pursuit of heresy by confiscating the goods of those accused. In the popular imagination, inquisitors were robbers who exploited their victims to line their own pockets. The reality was that for much of its existence the debts of the Holy Office outweighed its profits. Between 1480 and 1550 all of the Inquisition's financial operations, including the payment of salaries and the support of its infrastructure, were administered by the Crown. In return it collected all the income acquired through the confiscation of property and goods of those accused of heresy, as well as fines and penalties imposed for lesser offences. Between 1488 and 1497 around 83,500 ducats' worth of property belonging to Judaizers was seized in Andalusia (Alpert, 2001, p. 23). The rehabilitation and exile of Jewish offenders also provided the Crown with a sizeable income. In October 1509 Judaizers condemned in two regions of Andalusia were allowed to emigrate to the New World upon payment of 40,000 ducats to the royal treasury. However, ordinary revenues from confiscations soon proved insufficient to defray the expenses of the expanding inquisitorial bureaucracy since the majority of the accused were of humble means and the turnover of prisoners was irregular.

By the mid-sixteenth century it was evident that the Crown could no longer maintain the Holy Office. In 1550 Charles V and Inquisitor General Valdés agreed that the institution would henceforth manage its own finances. Valdés had to find reliable sources of income for each tribunal that would supply the necessary revenue to support the work of the Inquisition. Between 1556 and 1571 agreements (*concordias*) were reached to levy an annual tax on the principal *morisco* communities in the peninsula with the aim of providing funds for those tribunals under whose jurisdiction they lived. In exchange, Valdés promised not to confiscate the property of any *morisco* who was arrested. These arrangements held until the final expulsion of the *moriscos* in 1609, when their contribution amounted to 42.7 per cent and 48 per cent respectively of the Holy Office's income in Valencia and Zaragoza. In this way the *moriscos* of the kingdom of Aragón in particular helped to maintain the very tribunal that hounded them on account of their practice of an alien culture (Kamen, 1965, p. 520). The most profitable source of inquisitorial income was derived from an agreement made with the papacy in 1559 which allowed for the income from a total of 54 cathedral and 47 collegiate church canonries in Spain to be reserved for inquisitors (without residence). For the next two centuries confiscations and canonries remained the chief direct source of income for each tribunal, without which the Inquisition would have gone bankrupt. Nevertheless, the regular state of income of the majority of tribunals (part of which went to supporting the work of the Council) remained precariously balanced.

The annual income of the tribunal of Córdoba in the mid-seventeenth century was 3.5 million *maravedis*. Forty per cent of this income derived from the three canonries that pertained to the tribunal in Córdoba, Jaén and Ubeda. Out of this gross figure it had to pay the salaries of local inquisitors, which rose from 100,000 *maravedis* per annum in 1567 to 250,000 *maravedis* in 1603 and took up to 75 per cent of its income, as well as contribute to the operation of the *Suprema* in Madrid (accounting for up to 20 per cent of its income). In addition, it was required to finance the staging of *autos de fe*. The one held in Córdoba in 1665 cost 2 million *maravedis*. As a result, the tribunal found itself permanently in debt: in 1624 its expenditure exceeded income by over 26 per cent. In order to guarantee a regular income, local tribunals invested in ground rents (*censos*), bought from the proceeds of confiscations, which yielded a return of around 7 per cent per year in the late sixteenth century and were the most profitable form of revenue at the Inquisition's disposal. Land and house rents derived from property confiscations made up 76 per cent of the tribunal of Granada's income in 1573 (Kamen, 1965, p. 516). Despite this, the Inquisition never became a wealthy property-owning institution as was the case with the Church and military orders. It therefore cannot be said to have contributed to the economic decline of Spain in the seventeenth century, although it is certain that via its confiscations the prosperity of the *converso* community, who were most active in finance and industry, suffered a serious setback (Kamen, 1997, pp. 148–57; Martínez-Millán, 1987, pp. 159–70).

Appendix
Inquisitors General of Castile and Aragón, 1483–1818

Inquisitor General	Date of papal commission	Career
Tomás de Torque-mada, OSD	17 Oct 1483	Prior Segovia; Royal Confessor
Diego de Deza, OSD	1 Sep 1499	Bp Zamora (1494); Bp Salamanca (1494); Bp Jaen (1498); *Bp Palencia* (1500); *Abp Seville* (1504); Royal Confessor
Francisco Jiménez de Cisnersos, OSF	5 June 1507	*Abp Toledo* (1495–1517); Royal Confessor
Adrian of Utrecht	14 Mar 1518	Tutor Charles V; Bp Tortosa (1516); Gov Castile; Elected Pope Adrian VI (1522)
Alonso Manrique de Lara	10 Sep 1523	Bp Badajoz (1499); Bp Córdoba (1516); *Abp Seville* (1523–38)
Juan Pardo de Tavera	7 Nov 1539	Bp Ciudad Rodrigo (1514); Bp Osma (1523); Abp Santiago (1524); Pres Council Castile (1524); Pres Chancillería Valla-dolid (1524); *Abp Toledo* (1534–45)
Juan García de Loaysa, OSD	18 Feb 1546	Cllor Inq (1522); Bp Osma (1524); Bp Sigüenza (1532); Pres Cl Indies; Abp Seville (1539–46)
Fernando de Valdés y Salas	20 Jan 1547	Cllor Inq (1525); Bp Orense (1530); Bp Oviedo (1532); Bp León (1539); Bp Sigüenza (1539); Pres Cl Castile (1539); Cl State; *Abp Seville* (1546–68)
Diego de Espinosa	8 Sep 1566	Cllor Inq (1564); Cl State; Cl Indies; Pres. Cl Castile (1565); *Bp Sigüenza* (1568–72)
Pedro Ponce de León	7 Dec 1572	Cllor Inq (1547); Bp Ciudad Rodrigo (1550); Bp *Plasencia* (1560–73)

The Inquisition as an Institution 45

Gaspar de Quiroga	20 Apr 1573	Cllor Inq (1566); Pres Cl Italy (1567); *Bp Cuenca* (1571–7); Cl State (1574); *Abp Toledo* (1577–94)
Jerónimo Manrique de Lara	1 Aug 1595	Cllor Inq (1575); Bp Cartagena (1583); Bp Avila (1591–5)
Pedro de Portocarrero	1 Jan 1596	Bp Calahorra (1589); Bp Córdoba (1594); *Bp Cuenca* (1597–9)
Fernando Niño de Guevara	11 Aug 1599	Pres Cl Castile (1546); Cl State; *Abp Seville* (1601–9)
Juan de Zúñiga	29 Jul 1602	Cllor Inq (1586); Cl State; Pres Cl Italy; Bp Cartagena (1600–2)
Juan Bautista de Acevedo	20 Jan 1603	*Bp Valladolid* (1601–6); Pres Cl Castile (1616)
Bernardo de Sandoval y Rojas	12 Sep 1608	Bp Ciudad Rodrigo (1586); Bp Pamplona (1588); Bp Jaen (1596); Cllor State; *Abp Toledo* (1599–1618)
Luis de Aliaga Martínez, OSD	4 Jan 1619	Cllor Inq (1614); Royal Confessor; Cl State
Andrés Pacheco	12 Feb 1622	Bp Segovia (1587); Bp Cuenca (1601–22)
Antonio de Zapata y Mendoza	30 Jan 1627	Bp Cádiz (1587); Bp Pamplona (1596); Bp Burgos (1600–4); Cl State
Antonio de Sotomayor, OSD	17 Jul 1632	Royal Confessor; Cl State; Cllor Inq (1622)
Diego de Arce y Reinoso	18 Sep 1643	Bp Tuy (1635); Bp Avila (1638); *Bp Plasencia* (1640–9); Cl Castile
Pascual de Aragón	26 Oct 1665	*Abp Toledo* (1666–77)
Juan Everardo Nitard, SJ	15 Oct 1666	Royal Confessor; Cl State
Diego Sarmiento de Valladares	15 Sep 1669	Cllor Inq (1661); Pres Cl Castile (1668); Bp Oviedo (1668); *Bp Plasencia* (1668–77)
Juan Tomás de Rocaberti, OSD	2 Aug 1695	Viceroy and *Abp Valencia* (1677–99)
Alonso Fernández de Córdoba y Aguilar	Sep 1699**	Cllor State. Died 19 Sep 1699
Baltasar de Mendoza y Sandoval	31 Oct 1699	*Bp Segovia* (1699–1727)

46   The Inquisition as an Institution

Continued

Inquisitor General	Date of papal commission	Career
Vidal Marín	24 Mar 1705	Bp Ceuta
Antonio Ibáñez de la Riva Herrera	5 Apr 1709	*Abp Zaragoza* (1687–1710)
Francisco Giudice	11 Jun 1711	
José Molines	Jan 1717**	
Diego de Astorga y Céspedes	26 Mar 1720	Bp Barcelona (1716–20)
Juan de Camargo y Angulo	18 July 1720	*Bp Pamplona* (1716–25)
Andrés de Orbe y Larreategui	28 July 1733	*Abp Valencia* (1725–38)
Manuel Isidro Manrique de Lara	1 Jan 1742	*Abp Santiago* (1738–45)
Francisco Pérez de Prado y Cuesta	22 Aug 1746	*Bp Teruel* (1732–55)
Manuel Quintano Bonifaz	11 Aug 1755	
Felipe Beltrán	27 Feb 1775	*Bp Salamanca* (1763–83)
Agustín Rubin de Cevallos	17 Feb 1784	*Bp Jaen* (1780–93)
Manuel Abad y la Sierra	11 May 1793*	
Francisco Antonio de Lorenzana	12 Sep 1794	*Abp Toledo* (1772–1800)
Ramón José de Arce y Reynoso	1798	*Bp Burgos* (1797–1801); *Abp Zaragoza* (1801–16)
Francisco Xavier Mier y Campillo	Aug 1814*	*Bp Almería* (1801–16)
Gerónimo Catellón y Salas	Oct 1818*	*Bp Tarazona* (1815–35)

Notes:

1 Italicized offices of archbishop or bishop held in conjunction with that of Inquisitor General.

2 * Dates of possession of office.

3 ** Confirmed in office but died before taking possession.

Sources: Lea, 1922), I, pp. 556–9; Martínez-Millán and Sánchez Rivilla, 1984, pp. 71–123; *Diccionario de Historia Eclesiástica de España*, (eds) Q. Aldea, T. Marín, J. Vives, 4 vols (Madrid: CSIC, 1972–5).

3 The Inquisition and the *Converso*

The Spanish Inquisition was originally established to deal with a specific group of individuals known as *conversos* – Jews who had voluntarily converted to Christianity and were commonly regarded as being insincere in their new faith and secretly reverting to their former one. At the beginning of the reign of Ferdinand and Isabella, backsliding Jews were considered to be a potential threat to the stability of the new Catholic state, recently emerged from the long years of struggle against Moorish occupation and eager to assert its dominance as both a political and a religious force. Such was the monarchs' concern, that a special institution – the Holy Office of the Inquisition – was established to root out the incidence of heresy within *converso* society. The Inquisition became universally synonymous with the intolerance and brutality directed at the crypto-Jewish community of urban Spain. This reputation was to dominate the tribunal's whole history, although it represented only a small percentage of its overall activity.

Anti-semitic Tensions in Spanish Society

The Jewish community, persecuted in and then expelled from most other parts of western Europe between the late thirteenth and mid-fourteenth centuries, remained tolerated and highly valued in Spain. Although barred from holding public office and forced to live in segregated zones (known as *aljamas*), the Jews made a valuable professional and cultural contribution to Spanish society. Some established reputations as doctors, tax collectors and financiers, others worked as artisans and traders. Social and economic factors, rather than religious or racial ones, were initially responsible for a change in public attitude towards them. Protected by their separate existence, their wealth and their influence with Peter I of Castile (1350–69) and the aristocracy, the Jews escaped the widespread suffering and turmoil brought about by the Black Death in the mid-fourteenth century. But their fortunes were soon to decline under the turbulent three decades of rule by the Trastámara dynasty that followed. Popular feelings of indignation at the Jews' superior social and economic status, inflamed through provocative sermons, found their expression in anti-semitic riots in major Castilian and Aragonese towns in 1391 (Wolff, 1971, pp. 4–18).

Following these disturbances, more than half the original Jewish population of around 200,000 (three-quarters of whom were settled in Castile) chose to convert to Christianity rather than to suffer continuing persecutions and threats to their livelihoods. They became known as *conversos* or New Christians. The dramatic reduction in size of Jewish communities in towns such as Seville, Toledo, Burgos, Segovia and Valladolid was matched by a corresponding increase in the number of *converso* inhabitants. During the first half of the fifteenth century former Jews were easily absorbed into a tolerant Christian culture that accepted them as equals. Although conversion was not obligatory at this stage, it increasingly became advisable in order to survive. While the Jew continued to be subject to legal and social discrimination, deemed responsible for all the evils afflicting the realm, major honours and offices remained open to the *converso*. Many converts rose rapidly under royal protection to occupy highly respectable positions within the Church, at Court, in finance and administration, while also maintaining amicable relations with their Jewish kin. However, their critics regarded them as unscrupulous opportunists.

In the second half of the fifteenth century, as the sincerity of the *converso*'s religious conviction was placed under ever closer scrutiny, Jewish converts to Christianity became increasingly marginalized. *Conversos* were widely believed to be public Christians but private Judaizers. Just how valid this perception was is difficult to judge. There appears to have been at best a mixture of loyalties and a complexity of religious attitudes within *converso* society: while some embraced Christianity fully others remained Jewish in all but name. In the face of mounting repression and enforced segregation, many were obliged to lead double lives, conforming to the dominant culture in public and reaffirming their Jewish faith and ties of kinship in private. The royal chronicler at the court of Ferdinand and Isabella, Fernando del Pulgar, who was himself of Jewish origin, related how a diversity of beliefs could be found within the same *converso* household, with genuine converts living alongside others who were secretly or openly reverting to the faith of their forefathers: 'And it happened that in some households the husband kept certain Jewish ceremonies and the wife was a good Christian, and that one son and daughter might be good Christians while another son was of the Jewish faith' (Cantera Burgos, 1972, p. 347). Very little effort appears to have been made by the Church authorities to instruct the *converso* into the Christian religion. Jews and Jewish converts remained in contact with one another, thus maintaining the old spirit of *convivencia* or peaceful co-existence.

In the eyes of Christian society, a Jew revealed himself by his social and dietary habits, such as the keeping of the Sabbath, speaking and reading in Hebrew, the continued practice of Jewish ceremonies within the family, the eating of unleavened bread and a refusal to eat bacon or pork, rather than in his explicit rejection of Christian doctrine. It was evidence of this nature that was later to be used by the Spanish Inquisition as indicative of the 'heretical' inclinations of the accused. According to some contemporary Jewish historians (notably Benzion Netanyahu and Norman Roth) inquisitors deliberately made up this evidence to incriminate the crypto-Jew, revealing their own anti-semitic prejudices, while other scholars (such as Yitzhak Baer and Haim Beinart) argue that the *converso* was indeed guilty of religious backsliding.

Beinart's publication of records of the trials of *conversos* brought before the tribunal of Ciudad Real in 1484 reveals examples of the suspicions surrounding former Jews. María González was the first *conversa* to be sentenced to death by burning by the local tribunal for leading a double life as a Judaizer. She was accused along with her husband Juan of keeping the Sabbath, wearing best clothes on Saturdays, saying Jewish prayers, lighting an oil lamp on Friday evenings, bringing up their children as Jews, and eating unleavened bread and meat during Lent. She confessed in October during the Period of Grace that it was her husband who had made her keep Jewish law but that now she went to church and confessed with her children. The prosecution doubted the sincerity of her confession. Many witnesses testified that the family had kept the Jewish law and the local priest confirmed that she had only been to church in the last two years (Beinart, 1974, pp. 70–90). Juan Falcón the elder also belonged to the same network of *converso* families in late fifteenth-century Ciudad Real. He admitted to town councillors (*regidores*) at a council meeting that he still practised Judaism. He lit oil lamps and prepared food for the Sabbath on Friday, ate unleavened bread and drank Jewish wine. He wore clean clothes and rested on the Sabbath, invited others to his house to read and say prayers in Hebrew, ate meat during Lent and slaughtered according to Jewish law and denied the existence of heaven and hell. Thirty-nine witnesses, including two of his sons, testified for the prosecution. He was tried post-humously, his bones exhumed and burnt in an *auto de fe* held in March 1485 (Beinart, 1974, pp. 551–67).

The Statutes of *Limpieza de Sangre*

In 1449, in the wake of further anti-semitic tensions in Toledo, all those of Jewish ancestry, however sincere and long-standing their conversion to Christianity, were barred from holding municipal office in the city by means of a civic law, known as the 'Sentence Statute' or *Sentencia Estatuto*. The Toledan statute was insti-gated in response to a violent power struggle that was taking place between *converso* and non-*converso* families within a city once renowned for its climate of multi-cultural co-operation (Sicroff, 1985, pp. 51–6). Jewish converts were resented for the monopoly they held over public office and for being so successful in their enterprises that they threatened the careers and live-lihoods of the Old Christian community. The Toledan statute established an important discriminatory code, soon to be adopted by other secular and religious institutions, one based on race rather than exclusively on religion. This code, known as *limpieza de sangre* (purity of blood), confirmed the commonly held belief that the *converso* was a suspect, second-class citizen. To be of pure Old Christian ancestry was soon to become the essential prerequisite for social advancement and acceptability. A clear precedent of exclusion had been set which the Inquisition was subsequently to reinforce.

THE *SENTENCIA ESTATUTO* OF PERO SARMIENTO, TOLEDO, 5 JUNE 1449

We must and do declare, must pronounce and do pronounce and constitute and ordain and command that all the said converts, descendants of the perverse lineage of the Jews, in whatever guise they may be, both by virtue of canon and civil law, which determines against them in the matter declared above [exclusion from public office], and by virtue of the privilege given to this city by the said lord king of blessed memory, Don Alfonso, king of Castile and Leon, progenitor of the king our lord, and by other lords and kings their progenitors, and by his highness [the present king], sworn and confirmed as follows:

Since by reason of the heresies and other offences, insults, seditions and crimes committed and perpetrated by them up to this day ... they should be had and held as the law has and holds them, as infamous, unable, incapable and unworthy to hold any office and public or private benefice in the said city of Toledo and in its land, territory and jurisdiction, through which they might have lordship over Christians who are old believers in the holy Catholic faith of Our Lord Jesus Christ, to do them harm and injury, and thus be infamous, unable and incapable to give testimony on oath as public scribes or as witnesses, following the tenor and form of the said privileges, liberties, franchises and immunities of the said city, we deprive them, and declare them to be and order that they be deprived of whatever offices and benefices they have had and held in this said city, in whatever manner.

Source: Benito Ruano, 1976, pp. 89–90 (trans. Edwards, 1994, pp. 100–1)

However, at this early stage, discrimination against the *converso* was still not widely exercised or accepted, remaining largely confined to major towns. There was, indeed, considerable opposition to Toledo's anti-semitic legislation, notably within senior religious circles where it was deemed to be an act of supreme intolerance. Following papal condemnation of the *Sentencia* as contrary to Christian principles, a number of prominent *conversos*, including the Dominican friar Juan de Torquemada (uncle of the first Inquisitor General of Spain) and the Bishop of Burgos, Alonso de Cartagena, declared themselves in writing to be opposed to the statute. In 1465 the General of the Jeronimites, Alonso de Oropesa, who actively encouraged Judaizers to become members of his Order, also intervened in the debate. By the end of the fifteenth century there was ample evidence of the successful professional, social and cultural assimilation of the *converso* into Old Christian society despite the growing impact of the purity of blood laws. Many converts to Christianity married into aristocratic circles where they formed powerful, expanding family alliances. Ferdinand himself was reputed to be of *converso* stock. A number of Castilian bishops were of known Jewish descent in the second half of the fifteenth century, including Juan Arias de Ávila, Bishop of Segovia (1461–97) and Alfonso de Burgos, Bishop of Córdoba (1477–82), Cuenca (1482–5) and Palencia (1485–99). But the forces of tolerance were never that far removed from those of intolerance.

Despite the widespread criticism that the Toledan civic statute of 1449 generated, the movement soon gathered momentum. Statutes were first adopted by specific secular institutions (university colleges, guilds and town councils) in the second half of the fifteenth century, then by selective cathedral chapters and religious orders in the sixteenth. In 1547 the Archbishop of Toledo, Juan Martínez Silíceo (1546–57), forced his cathedral chapter – heavily infiltrated by men of *converso* origin – to adopt its own exclusive entry test. All those seeking preferment were now obliged to have their ancestry checked over four generations for any trace of Jewish lineage. A further requirement was for the candidate not to be related to anyone who had been found guilty by the Inquisition, a stain that branded whole families with infamy. At the same time, Silíceo was also demonstrating that although himself of lowly background, he was superior to those with tainted blood. In a highly competitive society, proof of *limpieza de sangre* thus became an important symbol of status and honour for the ordinary man or woman, hence its popular appeal. The Inquisition's own position in relation to purity of blood remained, ironically perhaps, somewhat ambiguous: it did not totally exclude *conversos* as employees until 1572 (Elliott, 1983, pp. 221–3; Kamen, 1993b, VII, p. 3) (see table 3.1).

Religious and racial tensions continued to be motivated in part by prevailing social and economic conditions. The second half of the fifteenth century was characterized by a series of prolonged subsistence crises in Castile, the most serious taking place over the period 1465–73 and coinciding with the political anarchy that marked the end of the reign of Henry IV (MacKay, 1972, pp. 33–67). In these popular uprisings anti-converso tensions ran high, reaching their climax in 1473 when a series of massacres of converted Jews took place in a number of Andalusian towns. The Jewish convert was victimized (as his forefathers had been at the end of the fourteenth century), not specifically for his race or his suspect religion, but on account of his social and professional advancement that enabled him to escape the worst effects of the crisis that so crippled the populace. Against this background of

Table 3.1   Institutions adopting *limpieza de sangre* statutes, 1482–1547

1482	The *Colegio Mayor* of San Bartolomé, University of Salamanca
1483	The Holy Inquisition (episcopal inquisitors)
1483	The Military Order of Alcántara
1483	The Military Order of Calatrava
1486	The Jeronimite Order
1488	The *Colegio Mayor* of Santa Cruz, University of Valladolid
1511	The Cathedral Chapter of Badajoz
1515	The Cathedral Chapter of Seville
1519	The *Colegio Mayor* of San Ildefonso, University of Alcalá
1525	The Franciscan Order
1527	The Military Order of Santiago
1530	The Cathedral Chapter of Córdoba
1531*	The Dominican Order (*onwards)
1537	The University of Seville
1547	The Cathedral Chapter of Toledo

Sources: Kamen, 1997, pp. 233–6; Domínguez Ortiz, 1957, pp. 57–68

indiscriminate attack on the *converso* community, the Jews, although marginalized in major cities and subject to heavy taxation, continued to practise their faith and remained under the official protection of the Crown. Jews held important roles at Court as royal financiers, tax collectors, physicians and advisers. Among the most prominent were Abraham Senior, the chief rabbi of Castile and principal treasurer to the Crown, and Luis de Santángel, secretary to the king. On the eve of Ferdinand and Isabella's reign, the Jews' contribution to society was clearly valued and their expulsion was certainly not high on the immediate political agenda. Nevertheless, there were obvious anomalies between the position of Jews and of Jewish converts in Spanish society that had to be resolved.

TEST OF PURITY OF BLOOD FOR ADMITTANCE TO OFFICE WITHIN THE INQUISITION OF CUENCA: QUESTIONS TO BE ANSWERED BY WITNESSES

1   Firstly, if they know the said —— concerning whom this inquiry is proceeding. The witnesses are to declare the basis of their knowledge [of the person] and over what period of time it extends.

2   *Item*, they must declare if they know, or knew —— and ——, the father and mother of the said —— and if they know the place where they were born, and where they have since lived, and where they now reside. The witnesses are to declare the basis of their knowledge and to give a full account of it.

3   *Item*, they must declare if they know, or knew —— and —— the father and mother of the said ——, paternal grandparents of the said ——, and if they know of any other forebears of the father of the said ——, where they were born and where they have been resident and where they now live. The witnesses are to declare the basis of their knowledge and over what period of time it extends.

4   *Item*, they must declare if they know, or knew —— and —— father and mother of the said ——, maternal grandparents of the said ——, and if they know of any forebears of the mother of the said ——, where they were born and where they have been resident and where they now live. The witnesses are to declare the basis of their knowledge and over what period of time it extends.

5   *Item*, they are to be asked certain questions prescribed by law, such as whether they are in debt to, are related to, or are enemies of the above-mentioned, or any one of them, whether they have been intimidated or suborned to speak other than the truth.

6   *Item*, they are to declare that ——, about whom this inquiry concerns, is deemed to be the legitimate son of the aforementioned ——, and the witnesses should declare how they know this to be the case.

7   *Item*, they are to declare whether they know if the said —— and his said father and said paternal grandparents, each and every one of them, have been and are Old Christians, of pure blood, without any stain or taint of Jewish, Moorish or *Converso* origins, or of any other newly converted sect. They are to declare that such persons have been and continue to be commonly held in good reputation, that on the contrary they have not been the subject of notoriety or rumour, and if it be the case that the witnesses know of it or have heard it reported through their own knowledge and information gleaned on the said person.

8   *Item*, they are to declare whether they know if the said —— or his said father, or his said paternal grandparents and other forebears have been condemned or subjected to penances by the Holy Office, or have fallen into any other notoriety that would prevent the holding of rank and public office; the witnesses are to say and declare all they know about these matters and about the virtuous habits, opinions and prudence exhibited by the said ——.

9   *Item*, they are to declare whether they know that the said —— mother of the said —— and the maternal grandparents of the said —— and all other forebears on the mother's side, each and every one of them, have been and are Old Christians, of pure blood, without any stain or taint of Jewish, Moorish or *Converso* origins, or of any other newly converted sect. They are to declare that such persons have been and continue to be commonly held in good reputation, and that such is the public voice, rumour and general opinion; that on the contrary they have not been the subject of rumour or notoriety, and that it be the case that the witnesses know of or have heard it reported through their own knowledge and information gleaned on the said person.

10 *Item*, they are to declare whether they know that —— mother of the said —— and the said parents and grandparents on the mother's side and other antecedents have been condemned or subjected to penalties by the Holy Office, or fallen into any disgrace or notoriety which would prevent the said —— from holding public office.

11 *Item*, they are to declare whether they know that the said candidate through any of the family lines cannot prove his lineage on the basis of the three tests, via grandparents, brother of grandparents, and extending to the son or grandchild of the grandparent's brother.

Continues

Continued

12 *Item*, they are to declare that they know the said —— to be of peaceful nature, not part of any faction or feud and whether they know if the said candidate is too much given to the swearing of oaths and if he has readopted clerical status, and what property he owns, the neighbourhood he lives in and how many familiars there are currently in the area.

13 *Item*, they are to declare that all of the aforesaid is publicly known and whether they know the other witnesses to be Old Christians and persons who will speak the truth under oath.

Source: Jiménez Monterserín, 1980, pp. 624–6 [translated by HR]

The Beginnings of the Spanish Inquisition

Following the quelling of the Andalusian pogroms, a number of senior churchmen, including two powerful members of the Dominican Order – the royal preacher, Alonso de Hojeda, and the royal confessor, Tomás de Torquemada – began to press for the establishment of a Spanish Inquisition. The opportunity came when the monarchs made an official visit to the city of Seville (1477–8) wherein was housed a prominent *converso* community. Hojeda and Torquemada, with the support of Cardinal Pedro González de Mendoza, Archbishop of Seville (1474–82), persuaded Ferdinand and Isabella of the danger posed by this offensive religious minority in their midst. The Queen, a deeply pious woman, totally committed to the Catholic cause, was shocked by their revelations of *converso* treachery and became convinced of the need to set up the appropriate secular machinery for the detection and punishment of heresy. In November 1478 Sixtus IV gave his formal consent for Ferdinand and Isabella to establish a Spanish Inquisition to deal with the perceived threat to the Catholic identity of their kingdoms posed by backsliding Jews. The institution was to be modelled on that set up by the papacy in the thirteenth century in the neighbouring Crown of Aragón to deal with the problem of Catharism. Unlike its Aragonese equivalent (now fallen into disuse), the Spanish Inquisition was to operate under the monarchs' direct control, thus extending their political authority over their Church (formerly responsible for heresy) and their spiritual authority over their people. Two years later, in September 1480, the Spanish Inquisition began its operations in Seville under the supervision of two Dominican inquisitors. The first *auto de fe* was held in the city on 6 February 1481 at which six prominent *conversos* were condemned to death at the stake (Hillgarth, 1978, II, pp. 422–4; Kamen, 1997, pp. 43–5).

A CONTEMPORARY ACCOUNT OF HOW HERESY WAS DEALT WITH IN SEVILLE, C.1480.

And he gave principal charge of this Inquisition to a friar of upright life who had great zeal in the Faith, who was called Fray Tomas de Torquemada, confessor to the king and prior of the monastery of Santa Cruz of Segovia of the Order of St Dominic. This prior, who was the chief inquisitor, put other inquisitors in his place in all the other cities and towns of the kingdom of Castile, and Aragon, and Valencia, and Catalonia. These made inquisitions on the matter of heretical iniquity in every land and district where they were assigned; and in these places they set their charters and edicts, founded upon law, so that those who had engaged in Jewish practices or who were not in accord with the Faith, within a certain time might come to confess their faults and be reconciled with Holy Mother Church. And by these charters and edicts many persons of lineage, within the term that had been set, appeared before the inquisitors and confessed their faults and the errors that they had committed in this crime of heresy. And these were given penances according to the degree of the crime that each one had incurred. These were more than fifteen thousand persons, men as well as women. And if some were guilty of that crime and did not come to be reconciled within the period of time that had been decreed, once there was information from witnesses of the error they had committed, then they were taken prisoner and trial was instituted against them, by means of which they were condemned as heretics and apostates and turned over to secular justice.

   Up to two thousand men and women were burned on various occasions in different cities and towns; and others were condemned to perpetual imprisonment; and to others was given as a penance that for all the days of their lives they should go marked with great red crosses placed on their clothing, both on the breast and on the back. And they as well as their children were declared unfit for all public office or responsibility, and it was decreed that they could not carry or wear silk or gold or camlet, on pain of death.

Continues

Continued

Some relatives of the prisoners and the condemned protested, saying that the inquisition and procedure was rigorous beyond what it ought to be and that in the manner in which the trials were conducted and in the execution of the sentences the ministers and executors showed that they had hatred for those people. The king and the queen turned over this matter to certain prelates, men of conscience, who were to look into it and justly remedy the matter.

Source: Cantera Burgos, 1972, pp. 337–42

The rigours of the institution soon made their mark. Crypto-Jews were rooted out and spared no mercy. Pulgar reported that many Jews were prepared to inform on *conversos* for their betrayal of the Jewish faith. Likewise genuine converts sought to denounce false ones for bringing the whole of *converso* society into disrepute. Although the exact numbers of those burnt at the stake varies according to sources and has clearly been exaggerated by polemicists, there is no doubt that the Inquisition was at its most brutal during the opening decades of its existence. It has recently been estimated that around 2,000 people (75 per cent of all victims) died at the hands of the Inquisition during the period between 1480 and 1530. Two hundred and fifty *conversos* were condemned to death in person by the Toledan tribunal between 1485 and 1501, and 500 in effigy. Seven hundred were reportedly burnt at the stake in Seville during the first eight years of the tribunal's operations (1480–8) (Kamen, 1985, pp. 41–2; Kamen, 1997, pp. 59–60). In Córdoba, Inquisitor Diego Rodríguez Lucero sentenced 134 *conversos* to death over a six-month period between 1504 and 1505. His 'reign of terror' ended with his dismissal from office in 1508. Indeed, such was the severity of the Inquisition's activities during its early years that the papacy threatened to re-assert its authority over the institution. Against the background of these excesses, the machinery of the Inquisition expanded. Fifteen more regional tribunals were established throughout Spain in the period up to 1495 to join in the task of extirpating heresy from their realms (some of which were later suppressed or merged). A General Council of the Inquisition, known as the *Suprema*, was established in Madrid in 1483, presided over by the first Inquisitor General, the Dominican friar Tomás de Torquemada, to co-ordinate and control its operations in Castile and Aragón. His name was to become synonymous with the brutality and repression characteristic of the Inquisition's early history. By means of the Council, the two crowns became linked institutionally in pursuit of common religious objectives. But in the eastern kingdoms, the Inquisition had to overcome considerable resistance to its presence.

The Aragonese, who jealously guarded their kingdom's laws and liberties, strongly objected to being subject to Castilian inquisitorial authority. They already had their own inquisition (established in the thirteenth century but virtually inert by the mid-fifteenth) subject to papal jurisdiction. The Aragonese parliament complained to Ferdinand in 1484 that inquisitors (predominantly Castilian in origin), who had been appointed to investigate and punish heresy in Zaragoza, Huesca, Teruel, Lleida, Barcelona and Valencia, were threatening their liberties and privileges which the king had sworn to uphold (Monter, 1990, pp. 3–4). In addition to the constitutional argument, there were also fears that *converso* families, vital to the economic prosperity of the eastern kingdoms, would be driven out. Violent resistance erupted in the Aragonese capital, Zaragoza. In September 1485 the inquisitor Pedro Arubés was murdered before the high altar of Zaragoza cathedral. Crypto-Judaizers were singled out as the perpetrators of the crime. The Inquisition retaliated with a great sweep of convictions which effectively annihilated the Aragonese *converso* elite – its principal opponents. Thirty public *autos* were held in Zaragoza within three years of Arubés' murder. A total of 96 individuals were condemned to death by the tribunal between 1484 and 1492 on charges of Jewish heresy (Monter, 1990, pp. 11–15). *Conversos* were also rounded up by the neighbouring tribunals of Barcelona and Valencia. They made up over 90 per cent of its victims between 1484 and 1530 (Lea, 1922, I, pp. 592–611). At the beginning of the reign of Charles V, representatives of the Aragonese Corts meeting in Zaragoza petitioned the Crown for a reduction in the powers of the Inquisition which were impinging upon areas of local jurisdiction and for a moderation of its practices, including the use of torture. Complaints were also raised in Castile. In

THE DISTRICTS OF THE SPANISH INQUISITION 1570–1820

.... National boundaries

- - - District boundaries

⊙ Tribunal centres and dates of establishment

• Other towns

Map 1 Map of Inquisitorial Districts (adapted from Henry Kamen, *The Spanish Inquisition: An Historical Revision*, Yale University Press, 1997, p. 143)

1518, the session of the Castilian Cortes held in Valladolid asked their monarch to check that 'the office of the Holy Inquisition proceed in such a way as to maintain justice, and that the wicked be punished and the innocent not suffer'. Fifteen years later in Monzón, deputies protested that inquisitors were taking the definition of heresy beyond its natural limits (Kamen, 1997, pp. 76–80). Repeated complaints of unfair practice were raised over the course of the first half of the sixteenth century in both kingdoms, but to no avail. The Inquisition, despite its opponents, was fast becoming a vital institution, protected by both the Crown and the papacy, and tacitly supported by the vast majority of the Old Christian community whose values it reinforced.

We should also be aware that there were fundamental inconsistencies in the severity of punishment issued by regional tribunals. In the early years of the Inquisition's existence harsher penalties were imposed in New Castile and Valencia, for example, than in Catalonia, where there were fewer *conversos* and the Holy Office's powers were restrained by local autonomy laws (*fueros*). Inquisitors never set foot in certain areas of Galicia and the Basque country on account of their remoteness. The Toledan tribunal tended to issue New Christian artisans accused of adhering to Jewish religious practices with more severe punishments than those of higher social rank. Of the 1,641 *conversos* who had dealings with the Toledan Inquisition in 1495, the majority held relatively modest occupations such as jewellers and silversmiths, shoemakers, tailors and tradesmen. An analysis of trials of Judaizers brought before the Inquisition of Valencia between 1485 and 1530 has revealed similar findings: 90 per cent of those with identifiable professions were textile workers or merchants of moderate to poor means, suggesting that they were a target or vulnerable group (Hillgarth, 1978, II, pp. 413–14). John Edwards has demonstrated that when inquisitors visited the region of Soria in north-east Castile in 1486 and again in 1502 they typically found *conversos* guilty of 'crimes' of religious scepticism and irreverence. This scepticism did not necessarily imply either a rejection of Christianity or an affirmation of Judaism. Nor was it exclusive to the New Christian community, but rather symptomatic of the religious doubt that permeated much of Spanish, as well as European, society at the beginning of the early modern era (Edwards, 1988, pp. 3–25). When examined closely, the records of the Spanish Inquisition provide evidence of potential rather than actual incidence of Judaism among the *converso* community. Heresy was destined to remain a loose concept. But set against a background of latent socio-economic grievances in society, the penalties to be incurred for the secret practice of Judaism were skilfully brandished by the Crown in the closing decades of the fifteenth century to encourage denunciation, however flimsy the premise.

AN EDICT OF FAITH INVITING PEOPLE TO IDENTIFY JUDAIZERS IN THEIR MIDST (ADAPTED)

If you know or have heard of anyone who keeps the Sabbath according to the laws of Moses, wearing clean shirts and other new garments, and putting clean cloths on the table and clean sheets on the bed on feast-days in honour of the Sabbath, and using no lights from Friday evening onwards; or they have purified the meat they are to eat by bleeding it in water; or have cut the throats of cattle or birds they are eating, uttering certain words and covering the blood with earth; or have eaten meat in Lent and on other days forbidden by Holy Mother Church; or have fasted the great fast, going barefooted that day; or if they say Jewish prayers at night begging forgiveness of each other, the parents placing their hands on the heads of their children without making the sign of the cross or saying anything but, 'Be blessed by God and by me'; or they bless the table in the Jewish way; [...] Or if they recite the psalms without the *Gloria Patri*; or if any woman keeps forty days after childbirth without entering a church; or if they circumcise their children or give them Jewish names; or if after baptism they wash the place where the oil and chrism was put; [...] Or if anyone on his deathbed is turned to the wall to die, and when he is dead is washed with hot water, his hair shaved from all parts of his body; [...] Or if anyone has declared the law of Moses to be as good as that of our Lord Jesus Christ ... [may they declare it].

Source: Jiménez Monteserín, 1980, pp. 505–10 (translation in Kamen, 1997, p. 286)

The Expulsion of the Jews

While *conversos* suspected of reverting to their former faith were being arrested, tried and tortured at the hands of the Inquisition, it was clear that tolerance of Jews in Spanish society could not

long be sustained. Following a ruling issued by the Cortes of
Toledo in 1480 they were forced to live a segregated existence,
confined to urban ghettos (*aljamas*) where they were the victims
of various forms of social and fiscal discrimination. In Segovia,
Jews were not allowed to buy food during working hours or to
eat fish on Fridays, while in Medina del Campo they were
prohibited from participating in commercial activity in the
local market. In Burgos, Jewish midwives were not allowed to
attend to Christian women in childbirth. Any Jewish merchant
who slept overnight in the port of Bilbao was subject to a fine of
2,000 *maravedís*. The Jews, who formed 1 to 1.5 per cent of the
total Castilian population on the eve of their expulsion, contributed disproportionately to the tax burden, bearing responsibility
for up to 15 per cent of the total sum collected in certain bishoprics (Hillgarth, 1978, II, p. 443; MacKay, 1972, p. 36). As
Tomás de Torquemada took up office as Inquisitor General in
1483, a partial expulsion of Jews was authorized from the Andalusian dioceses of Seville, Córdoba and Cádiz. This was also
the frontier zone for the advancement of Christian forces on
Granada, amongst whom religious zeal ran increasingly high.
Three years later, a similar expulsion of Jews was ordered from
the Aragonese dioceses of Zaragoza, Albarracín and Teruel, but
without it taking immediate effect. Although the Inquisition
lacked the authority to condemn them for their beliefs, it was
indirectly forcing the Jewish community into an untenable position. The local expulsions were the prelude to a total expulsion.

 In November 1490 a group of six Jews and five *conversos* were
arrested and tried in Ávila under the watchful eye of Torquemada
for the kidnap and ritual murder of a young Christian boy from
the town of La Guardia, near Toledo (referred to as El Niño de La
Guardia). It was alleged that the kidnappers intended to remove
the heart from their victim whose blood they would employ for
magical purposes to destroy Christians. The trial was a showcase
that served to create in the popular imagination a larger-than-life
image of both the Jews (not officially subject to the jurisdiction of
the Inquisition) and the *conversos*, their co-religionists, as child
murderers, sorcerers and enemies of the Christian race. In November 1491 all those accused were found guilty and burnt alive at
the stake. The episode – later embellished by myth – added to the

anti-semitic tensions pervading Castile and may have put pressure on the monarchs to order a general expulsion of unconverted Jews from Castile and Aragón, carried out the following year (Haliczer, 1991, pp. 146–56; Edwards, 1999, pp. 83–5).

On 31 March 1492 a royal decree was issued which gave those Jews who refused Christian baptism four months in which to leave Spain or face the death penalty. The timing of the announcement seemed propitious. Christian Spain was triumphant following the fall of Granada and eager to affirm itself. Columbus was about to depart on his first voyage of discovery. The expulsion order gave Spaniards a further sense of achievement by removing the 'pernicious presence' of Judaizers, suspected of encouraging New Christians to revert to their old faith. Now Ferdinand and Isabella could truly claim to be the champions of Christendom and worthy of their title 'the Catholic Kings', bestowed upon them in 1494 by Pope Alexander VI in recognition of their services to Catholicism. There was some last-minute hesitation on the part of the Crown, which recognized the financial and professional losses likely to be incurred and perhaps foresaw the consequences of severing a cultural link that had its origins in Visigothic Spain. The Aragonese historian Jerónimo de Zurita warned his readers that 'many were of the opinion that the king was making a mistake to throw out of his realms people who were so industrious and hard-working, and so outstanding both in number and esteem as well as in dedication to making money. They also said that more hope could be entertained of their conversion by leaving them in the country than by throwing them out' (Kamen, 1992, p. 83). But anti-semitic pressure from below and the drive for religious unity from above were the overriding considerations that led to the publication of the edict of expulsion.

EDICT OF EXPULSION OF JEWS, 31 MARCH 1492

You well know, or should know, that because we were informed that in these our kingdoms there were certain bad Christians who judaised and apostasised from our holy Catholic faith, for which much of the reason was the communication by the Jews with the Christians, in the parliament that we caused to happen in the city of Toledo in the former year of

1480, we ordered that, in all the cities and towns and villages of our kingdoms and lordships, the Jews should be separated out where they lived, hoping that with their separation the problem would be solved. Also we had procured and ordered that an Inquisition should be made in our aforesaid kingdoms and lordships, which, as you know, was done more than twelve years ago and is still going on. It has discovered many guilty people, as is well known, and as we are informed by the inquisitors and by many religious people, ecclesiastical and secular, that a great danger to Christians has clearly emerged, this having followed, and still continuing from the activity, conversation [and] communication which [these Christians] have maintained with Jews. [These Jews] demonstrate that they always work, by whatever means they can, to subvert and remove faithful Christians from our holy Catholic faith, to separate them from it, and attract and pervert [them] to their wicked belief and opinion, instructing them in the ceremonies and observances of their Law. [...]

For this reason and to avoid and put an end to so great shame and offence to the Christian faith and religion, because every day it is found and becomes apparent that the said Jews increasingly pursue their bad and wicked project, wherever they live and converse [with Christians], and so that there should be no further occasion for offence to our holy faith ... [we have] to throw the said Jews out of our kingdoms.

And in this matter we order this our letter to be given, by which we give order to all Jews and Jewesses of whatever age they may be, who live and dwell in our aforesaid kingdoms and lordships... that by the end of the month of July coming, in this current year, they should leave all our aforesaid kingdoms and lordships, with their sons and daughters... and that they should not dare to return to them.

Source: Suárez Fernández, 1964, pp. 392–3 (trans. Edwards, 1994, pp. 49–51)

However, the decree of 'expulsion' also incorporated an open invitation to conversion. The Jews were to be given one last chance. As Andrés Bernáldez confirms in his early sixteenth-century chronicle: 'It was ordered that the holy Gospel and Catholic faith and Christian doctrine should be preached to all the Jews of Spain; and those who wished to convert and be baptized should remain in the realms as subjects, with all their goods' (Bernáldez, 1962, p. 251). The findings of new research suggest a much smaller exodus and a much larger number of conversions than has previously been calculated. The social and economic consequences of expulsion were correspondingly less severe than anticipated and are now judged to have had minimal impact on Spain's seventeenth-century decline. Using the baseline figure of some 80,000 Jews in Spain on the eve of their expulsion, according to the calculations of Henry Kamen, between the end of March and the end of July 1492 around 40,000–50,000 Jews left Spain (predominantly from Castile) for Portugal, Navarre and North Africa, while a similar number chose hasty baptism rather than enforced exile (Kamen, 1992, p. 85). Perhaps as many as 80 to 90 per cent of those who left Spain returned between 1493 and 1499 ready to accept the Christian faith in principle, but in practice uncertain of their real religious identity. The edict of 'expulsion' thus served to increase the number of reluctant converts and to exacerbate the *converso* problem within society. Although Judaism had been officially banned from Spain, Jewish influences were still deeply ingrained in Spanish society and their eradication was to prove to be no simple exercise. Despite their increasing marginalization, converted Jews continued to play an essential role in religious, intellectual and political life, trusted and resented in equal measure, long after the expulsion of their forefathers.

The Portuguese New Christians

Following the expulsion order of 1492 tens of thousands of Spanish Jews fled to Portugal rather than be forced into Christian baptism in their homeland. Although obliged to become converts in 1497, for most of the first half of the sixteenth century they lived in their adoptive land in relative freedom as crypto-Jews. They found themselves stigmatized, just as *conversos* were in Spain, but also valued for their skills, especially in cartography and navigation, vital to the success of the Portuguese voyages of exploration. When the Inquisition was established in Portugal in 1547, it agreed financial terms with the *cristaos-novos* in return for which they escaped severe punishment. During the first 33 years of its formal existence (1547–1580), just over 2,000 *conversos* were brought to trial by its tribunals – a relatively small number compared to the size of the problem they posed. The frequency with which pardons were issued to Portuguese New Christians who were widely suspected of Judaizing (in 1533, 1535, 1547 and 1577) suggests that the authorities preferred to leave them in peace to allow their commercial activities to prosper and thus enrich the economy. The arrangement also worked in reverse. The offer of money by New Christians to a permanently needy treasury smoothed the way towards the granting of pardons. But theirs was an existence of constant uncertainty (Alpert, 2001, pp. 31–4).

The Portuguese Inquisition suddenly became a much more repressive instrument of racial and religious control following the annexation of Portugal to Spain in 1580. Fifty *autos* were held in Lisbon, Evora and Coimbra between 1581 and 1600 at which 3,000 were penanced and 212 were condemned to death. This forced the New Christian community to seek alternative ways of preserving their ethnic identity and deploying their professional skills. Several thousand opted for migration to Castile, settling in commercial cities such as Madrid, Seville and Málaga, hoping for greater clemency from the Spanish as opposed to the Portuguese Inquisition. But this situation only endured while it suited the financial expediency of the monarch. In August 1604 a papal brief was issued which allowed over 400 Portuguese *conversos* to be released from inquisitorial custody and pardoned for past offences in exchange for a 1,860,000-ducat payment to Philip III. Those who fled to Spain under the terms of the pardon found ways of buying their freedom and protection (via loans to the treasury and bribes to ministers, including the Duke of Lerma). In turn the Crown was able to make use of their highly valued financial and entrepreneurial expertise to rescue its ailing economy (Kamen, 1997, pp. 287–9). In the years 1607, 1608, 1610 and 1611 no *conversos* came before the Spanish Inquisition. Shortly after all concessions granted to Portuguese *conversos* were withdrawn in 1610, the Holy Office, recently released from the pursuit of *morisco* heresy, once again began to root out the crypto-Jew.

The opening decades of the seventeenth century coincided with a fierce debate within the Inquisition and wider society over the continued need to apply the test of purity of blood. The *limpieza* statutes were regarded by many as unfairly discriminating against *conversos* whose family connections with Judaism in Spain were so remote as to be indiscernible, yet who continued to be treated as suspect Jews and barred from advancement in the professions (Kamen, 1993b, VII, pp. 1–29; Rawlings, 2002, pp. 139–42). Where Portuguese New Christians were concerned, however, their Jewish ancestry was more recent and therefore the test of *limpieza* could be applied with greater certainty. In 1619, Martín González de Cellorigo, an employee of the Inquisition of Toledo where he was in charge of confiscated property, wrote a *Plea for Justice* (*Alegación en que se funda la justicia*) in favour of Portuguese New Christians. He argued for their toleration less on religious than on financial grounds: the harnessing of their commercial expertise was vital to the interests of the Spanish economy (Alpert, 2001, pp. 42–5).

The financial crisis faced by Philip IV at the beginning of his reign forced him to give serious consideration to making use, as his father had done, of the entrepreneurial skills and capital of Portuguese New Christians, many of whom had fled Spain under the renewed round of persecutions. Although they brought new life to the practice of Jewish rites in the peninsula, most lived separately from the small Spanish *converso* community. Between 1626 and 1627 the Inquisition issued Portuguese financiers suspected of Judaic practices with a temporary pardon for past offences and allowed them to compete for financial contracts (*asientos*) with Italian bankers. The following year they were granted free access to trade anywhere within the Spanish Empire. By 1640 they were negotiating over 50 per cent of the loans required by the treasury to finance the debt payments of the Crown and support Spain's vast military effort overseas. They excelled as commercial transactors, collecting, making and moving money across international routes (Lynch, 1992, pp. 148–9). However, the protection offered to the New Christians, now acting as royal bankers, was a major source of scandal. In particular it raised the concerns of traditionalists within the Church who saw religious ideals being discarded to meet the financial expedients of a bankrupt government and exposed the underlying racial sympathies of the first minister, Olivares, who drew up a radical proposal in 1634 for exiled Jews to be able to return to Spain. The Spanish Inquisition never reconciled itself to the new deal for Portuguese *conversos* and maintained its vigilance over them in spite of government restraint and Philip IV's intervention to protect them from unnecessary harm: 'Considering how well I am served by these people and how satisfied I am with their good behaviour, I order that they be treated like other natives of these kingdoms and not as they have been treated up to now. They must not be vexed or harassed' (Alpert, 2001, p. 89).

On 4 July 1632 the Inquisition held a showcase *auto de fe* in the Plaza Mayor of Madrid. Six of the seven burned as Judaizers were of Portuguese origin. The event was accompanied by a widespread attack on the Crown's financiers. In 1630 Juan Núñez Saravía, a prominent Portuguese *asentista* (loans contractor), who had helped to negotiate a loan of over 2 million ducats for the Crown three years earlier, was denounced to the Inquisition of Toledo as a crypto-Jew. He emerged from six years of imprisonment in 1637, having been found guilty, forced to abjure on grave suspicions of heresy and fined 20,000 ducats. His career was ruined. Another leading Portuguese financier of the Crown, Manuel Fernández Pinto, was similarly convicted in 1636 and had 300,000 ducats' worth of goods confiscated from him (Kamen, 1997, pp. 291–2).

In 1640 Portugal re-asserted its independence from the Spanish monarchy and the Inquisition intensified its attack on the minority of Portuguese New Christians left in Spain – now its political adversaries. Once again, leading financiers who had previously served the Crown became the target of attack. Another member of the Saravía family, Diego de Saravía, was brought to trial in 1641 and was obliged to forfeit 250,000 ducats' worth of gold, silver and coin to the Inquisition. This was one example of many. Whole families were reportedly arrested in Madrid (often on the basis of false testimony) and many took flight. The diarist Jerónimo de Barrionuevo observed in June 1655 that 'The Cardosos have fled to Amsterdam, taking 200,000 ducats in wool and 250,000 in gold. It is said this was because the Inquisition wished to arrest them, and so they are in search of a land where one lives in greater freedom than in Spain.' In September of the same year he reported that 'Since last Saturday the Inquisition in Madrid has imprisoned seventeen Portuguese families. [. . .] In the street of the Peromostenses they are hurriedly building a prison big enough to hold all the people that fall every day into the trap. It is said for certain that there is not a Portuguese of high or low degree in Madrid who does not judaise' (Kamen, 1997, pp. 292–3). The flight of wealthy traders and bankers had inevitable consequences for the stability of the economy and led the Council of Finance to intervene in 1654 to protect the contracts of those accused. When the banker Fernando de Montesinos fled to Amsterdam to escape the wrath of the Inquisition, his business and property were left intact and his sons took up the role of Crown financiers. Sixty-one per cent of all the trials held by the Inquisition of Cuenca between 1650 and 1670 – where many of the cases denounced in Madrid were processed – were for the secret practice of Judaism. In Toledo the peak decade for the trial of Judaizers was 1651–60 when they accounted for 76.5 per cent of all cases, as compared with 12 per cent during the period 1601–10 (Alpert, 2001, pp. 91–2). By 1680, the rigorous pursuit of Portuguese New Christians had reached its climax. On 30 June of that year a grandiose *auto de fe* (depicted by the artist Francisco Rizi) was held in Madrid at which 56 Judaizers were 'reconciled' or severely punished and 22 sentenced to death by burning, the majority of Portuguese origin. *Autos de fe* after this date show a definite decline in *converso* victims. Although it seemed that by the end of the seventeenth century the first generation of Portuguese New Christians had effectively been wiped out, the Inquisition's work in this sphere was not over. During the opening decades of the eighteenth century it returned to its task of rooting out and punishing crypto-Judaism among the descendants of New Christians with renewed severity (see table 3.2).

During the period 1701–45 the Inquisition undertook its last major campaign against the descendants of Jews, the majority of whom were of Portuguese origin and the descendants of those persecuted in the mid-seventeenth century. Of all the crimes punished in *autos de fe* during this period, 1,149 (78.8 per cent of the total) were for Judaism, and of these 217 were burnt at the stake for their crime. The vast majority of the persecutions (950) occurred over the five-year period 1721–5, predominantly in

Table 3.2 Trials for Judaism in Castile, 1721–5

	1721	1722	1723	1724	1725
Madrid	14	11	—	20	—
Granada	48	48	108	38	27
Seville	38	82	35	41	10
Cuenca	31	18	1	8	10
Murcia	—	63	18	7	4
Córdoba	27	13	25	34	—
Valladolid	—	14	2	5	5
Toledo	—	44	6	—	5
Llerena	—	17	11	—	14
Total	158	310	206	153	75

Source: Kamen, 1985, p. 234

Castile (902), after which the number of cases declined considerably. Under threat of having its authority subordinated to the new Bourbon monarchy of Philip V, the Holy Office asserted itself and not for the first time in its history impressed its indispensability on the Crown. It sought out its traditional victims – middle-class lawyers, doctors, shopkeepers, tax farmers and their families – upon whom it took cruel revenge. All the old prejudices held against the *conversos* were revived to justify the hunt for and eradication of crypto-Judaism: their accumulation and secretion of wealth, their clandestine practice of Judaism and anti-Christian behaviour. As a result of this renewed backlash, the Inquisition enjoyed something of a political and financial revival during the opening decades of the century (Lynch, 1992, pp. 152–3). For one last time the Jewish enemy became the Inquisition's friend.

4 The Inquisition and the *Morisco*

The establishment of the Inquisition to eradicate the contagion of crypto-Judaism from Spain, and the enforced exile of those Jews who refused Christian baptism, changed the whole nature of multi-cultural relations in Spain. As Catholicism became the identifying symbol of Spanish nationhood, so the Moorish community found themselves in an increasingly vulnerable position. The Muslim problem was more complex and deep-rooted than the Jewish one. From an ideological standpoint, the Spanish Moor was looked upon less as a heretic than as a non-believer who could be persuaded into accepting the Christian faith. From a political standpoint, it was feared that he might lend his allegiance to the Ottoman Turk, particularly if he landed troops on the soil of . Spain. The capture of Constantinople in 1453 and the assembly of the Turkish fleet in the Black Sea and the Aegean in the 1470s augured a prolonged period of confrontation between Latin Christendom and Ottoman Islam. Given the almost eight century-long existence of the Moorish community within the peninsula and the potentially aggressive and expansive Ottoman empire, it was not surprising that Spain should have become more exigent over its Arab neighbours as the Reconquest came to an end. However, Spaniards still valued the Moors' contribution to society, in particular their economic one, hence the initial tolerance displayed towards Islam on its shores. The old enemy was also an old friend. This pre-condition was to underpin the whole relationship between the two cultures in the century after the last Moorish stronghold of Granada fell to the Christians in 1492 until the final expulsion of the Islamic community from Spain in 1609–14.

1492–1525: Co-existence and Conversion

There were two main geographical centres of Moorish habitation in the peninsula in 1492. In the eastern kingdom of Valencia, reconquered by the Christians in the thirteenth century, there was a Muslim population of around 160,000, making up 30 per cent of the local rural community. In the Nasrid kingdom of Granada in the south, the final bastion of Islam in Spain, there was a concentration of some 500,000 Moors. Although ultimately both communities suffered the same fate, their individual experiences of living under Christian rule were quite different, as was the chronology of their conversion and ultimate expulsion. Muslims living in eastern Spain worked as tenant farmers of the landed aristocracy. Their overlords valued them as hard-working labourers and respected their cultural identity. The Moors of Castile, including those of Granada, earned their living as small craftsmen: shoemakers, blacksmiths, carriers, muleteers, market gardeners, basket makers, tailors and joiners. As with their co-religionists in the east, they formed a vital labour force, prepared to live and work in conditions that were not acceptable to Old Christians. In both regions they lived in segregated communities, known as *morerías*, enjoying civil liberties but resented by Christians for their thriftiness, their sobriety and their separateness (Lynch, 1965, I, pp. 205–10).

At the end of the fifteenth century, it was the Granadine Moors who aroused most suspicion. This was due to the proximity of Granada to the North African coast and the potential for Turkish attack. Hence the priority that Ferdinand and Isabella attached at the beginning of their reign to seizing the kingdom of Granada and to bringing the War of Reconquest to an end. It seems that, at least initially, the monarchs were more concerned with establishing national unity and securing political stability along the vulnerable southern frontier than they were with imposing Catholicism on their Moorish subjects. We should not forget that they were simultaneously engaged in seeking a solution to the serious problem posed by Jewish converts in their kingdoms and it seems unlikely they would have wished to add to these. Indeed, very generous terms of surrender were negotiated with the Moors of Granada in 1491, prior to the Christian capture of the city in January 1492. The terms of the settlement, known as the *capitulaciones*, allowed for those Moors who chose to remain in Castile (some 200,000) to keep their language, customs, laws and property, as well as permitting them to practise their Islamic faith without interference, just as their ancestors (referred to as *mudéjares*) had done for centuries in the rest of Spain. The conciliatory terms of settlement granted to the vanquished Moors of Granada, which allowed for 'all the common people, great or small, to live in their own religion', suggests that religious uniformity was not an official priority at this stage.

THE *CAPITULACIONES* OF GRANADA, 1491 (EXTRACTS)

6. Their highnesses and their successors will ever afterwards allow King Abi Abdilehi and his *alcaides*, [judges], *muftis* [lawyers], *alguaciles* [judicial officials], military leaders, and good men, and all the common people, great or small, to live in their own religion, and not permit that their mosques be taken from them, nor their minarets nor their muezzins, nor will they interfere with the pious foundations or endowments which they have for such purposes, nor will they disturb the uses and customs which they observe.

19. King Bobadil and all his dignitaries, and all the common people of Granada, etc., would be well treated by their highnesses and their ministers, and that what they have to say will be listened to, and their customs and rites will be preserved, and all *alcaides* [*sic*] and *alfaquíes* will be allowed to collect their incomes and enjoy their pre-eminences and their liberties such as by custom they enjoy, and it is only right that they should continue to enjoy.

27. If any Moor were to go to North Africa and then find he did not like the way of life, he could return and have all the benefits of the *Capitulaciones*, so long as he returned within three years.

30. No Moor will be forced to become Christian against his or her will, and if for reasons of love an unmarried girl or a married woman or widow should wish to become Christian, she will not be received [into the church] until she has been questioned.

Source: Harvey, 1990, pp. 316–19

In the decade that followed, the traditional spirit of *convivencia* was revived largely through the activity of Hernando de Talavera, Archbishop of Granada (1493–1507). His strategy was one of conciliation: he made Christianity accessible to his new flock, not by using forceful or coercive tactics, but by adapting the faith to their needs. Known as 'the great *alfaquí* of the Christians', he set about learning Arabic and encouraged his clergy to do likewise. Muslim music replaced Christian music in many religious ceremonies. A converted Moor became a member of the Archbishop's household and his personal confessor. A fellow Jeronimite noted that Talavera 'detested the evil custom prevalent in Spain of treating members of the sects worse after their conversion than before' (Liss, 1992, p. 171). But the Archbishop's conciliatory approach was at once the measure of his success and the instrument of his downfall. His sympathy for and easy acceptance of the Moorish people and their culture raised doubts, later unsubstantiated, as to the purity of his own origins. By the end of the decade, Talavera's universal, tolerant approach to the delivery of Christianity was out of step with the increasingly intransigent religious policy of the Crown.

The year 1499 marked a major turning point in the Granada mission as Francisco Jiménez de Cisneros, Archbishop of Toledo (1495–1517), took charge of its direction. Increasing pressure and inducements, via sermons, bribes and threats, were placed on the Granadine Moors to abandon their cultural traditions and accept Christian baptism. This policy, which clearly violated the terms of surrender, prompted a series of uprisings against Cisneros' repressive measures. The atmosphere of trust between the majority and minority faiths now turned to one of mistrust, threatening the delicate balance of power within the kingdom. A revolt in the Albaicín district of Granada in December 1499 was followed in January by an armed struggle of three months' duration in the Alpujarras mountains outside the city. A programme of forced conversions, mass baptisms and the violent persecution of offenders of the faith followed. By the end of February 1500, there were a reported 50,000 new Moorish converts to Christianity in Granada – known as *moriscos* – but in the majority of cases theirs was nothing more than an outward show of conformity. The indiscriminate attack on Moorish culture culminated in

October 1501 with the ritual burning of thousands of precious Arabic manuscripts and books. A royal edict (known as a *pragmática*) was published on 12 February 1502, which bore all the hallmarks of that issued against the Jewish community ten years earlier. The Moors were now regarded as posing the same threat to the religious stability of Spain as the Jews had a decade before.

EDICT OF EXPULSION OF MOORS FROM CASTILE, 12 FEBRUARY 1502 (EXTRACT)

Considering ... that since the major cause of the subversion of many Christians that has been seen in these our kingdoms was their participation and communication with the Jews, that since there is much danger in the communication of the said Moors of our kingdom with the newly converted and they [the Moors] will be a cause that the said newly converted may be drawn and induced to leave our faith and to return to their original errors... as already by experience has been seen in some of this kingdom and outside of it, if the principal cause is removed, that is, to expel the said Moors from these our kingdoms and lordships, and because it is better to prevent with the remedy than to wait to punish the errors after they are made and committed ... it is right that they [the Moors] be expelled [from these kingdoms and lordships].

Source: Woodward, 1997, p. 82

The pragmatic required all non-baptized Moors to leave Castile and León within twelve months, thus bringing to an end almost eight hundred years of co-existence between the faiths in the kingdom. The majority chose to stay. By contrast, it was another quarter of a century before the Moors in the eastern kingdoms were required to submit to Christian baptism. In both regions the arrangement was a nominal one.

1526–1550: Respite

On a visit to Granada in 1526, Charles V was informed that 'the *Moriscos* are truly Moors: it is twenty-seven years since their conversion and there are not twenty-seven or even seven of them who are Christians' (Kamen, 1997, p. 221). In December of the

same year, following recommendations put forward by an ecclesiastical congregation, attempts were made to eradicate all
existing traces of a still flourishing Moorish civilization in Granada (including the use of Arabic, the dancing of the *zambra* and
the wearing of traditional Moorish dress). This task fell in part to
the Inquisition (established in Granada in 1526) which clearly
regarded an adherence to Islamic customs as an obstacle to the
acceptance of Christianity and therefore a punishable offence.
There thus evolved an assault by the Christian authorities, not
merely on the alleged religious deviance of the *morisco*, but on
his whole cultural identity, a culture which had flourished in
Spain for centuries and which was intimately interwoven with
his religious beliefs.

AN EDICT OF FAITH INVITING PEOPLE TO IDENTIFY MUSLIMS IN THEIR
MIDST (ADAPTED)

If you know of any people who say that Islam is the only route to
paradise and that Jesus Christ is not (the son of) God, but a prophet
and that he was not born of the Virgin; or if they have observed any
Islamic rites and ceremonies, such as keeping Friday as a holy day,
eating meat on days when it is prohibited by the Holy Catholic Church,
wearing clean clothes or special clothes on those days; or if they have
only eaten meat that has been slaughtered in the appropriate way; or if
they have given their children Moorish names; or if they have said that
there is no other God than Allah and Mahomet his messenger; or if
they have kept the fast of Ramadan, not taking any food or drink
during daylight hours; or if they have not eaten bacon or drunk wine in
accordance with Moorish custom; or if they have got married according to the Moorish rite and have sung their traditional songs and
performed traditional dances; or if they have buried their dead in
accordance with Islamic custom; or if they have admitted to getting
baptised without faith; or if they have said: 'bless your parents or
grandparents who died as Moors or Jews' or 'the Moor is saved by
his sect and the Jew by his laws' ... [may they declare it].

Source: Jiménez Monteserín, 1980, pp. 503–14 [translated by HR]

In practice, however, the *morisco* was able to maintain intact
his religious identity under the terms of the Muslim doctrine of
taqiyya (meaning precaution) which allowed him to adopt all the
appropriate external features of Christianity as long as he

remained privately faithful to Islam. His continued adherence to Islam (and therefore the falsity of his Christian belief) was revealed in his performance of daily prayer and his observance of periods of fast, most notably that of Ramadan, as well as his Sunday labours, his non-attendance at Mass, his feigning of confessional sins, his washing off of the chrism after baptism and his refusal to acknowledge the consecration of the eucharistic bread and wine. His preference for his native culture was, furthermore, identifiable in his whole way of life: in his dietary habits (such as his abstention from eating pork and drinking wine and his cooking with oil instead of lard), his attention to personal hygiene (engaging in ritual bathing on a Friday), his maintenance of group solidarity, his use of the Arabic tongue and his style of dress (García-Arenal, 1987).

The 1526 congregation also urged the local clergy to take greater responsibility for the integration of the *morisco* into the Christian Church via training programmes for priests and educative initiatives for parishioners. These proposals were never fully implemented. A financial compromise was reached by which Charles suspended the legislation and received payment of a large subsidy of 90,000 ducats over six years from the Granadine *moriscos*, principally derived from the profits of the silk industry, in return for which the local tribunal of the Inquisition exercised minimal vigilance over them. At the same time they remained protected by the Captaincy General of Granada, a hereditary office held in succession by three counts of Tendilla, members of the powerful aristocratic house of Mendoza, to whom the *moriscos* paid military taxes (known as the *fardas*) to support the cost of internal security in the region. Granadine Moorish converts were thus able to maintain virtually intact all the essential features of their cultural inheritance without fear of reprisal. A similar situation prevailed in the kingdom of Valencia where the *moriscos* were granted a 40-year period of grace from inquisitorial prosecutions in 1525 in return for a payment of 40,000 ducats to the Crown. The fact that the *moriscos'* nominal Christianity was quietly tolerated suggests that they were still valued for the contribution they made to society as skilled labourers, artisans and craftsmen – and, most importantly for the Crown, as taxpayers, which more than made up for the doubtful status of their conversion. The *modus vivendi* of Moorish society in Spain thus survived throughout most of the first half of the sixteenth century. The Church believed, even into the 1550s, that the *moriscos* were simple folk, ignorant of the faith, and that with time and vigilance they would abandon their old traditions (Lovett, 1986, pp. 258–60).

1560–1570: Coercion and Revolt in Granada

During the early 1560s, the Granadine *moriscos* became more restive as the terms of their immunity expired and the local tribunal of the Inquisition stepped up its activity against them. Ninety-two per cent of the prosecutions it mounted concerned *moriscos* in 1566 as compared with 50 per cent in 1550. It was now no longer possible to superficially satisfy the rules of conformity where the fulfilment of Christian ritual was concerned, as many had previously managed to do. Turkish advances in the western Mediterranean ocean, combined with corsair raids along the southern coast, compounded fears of the possible recapture of Granada. Pedro Guerrero, Archbishop of Granada (1546–76), recently returned from the Council of Trent, instructed his clergy, assembled in a Provincial Council between 1565 and 1566, to engage in a rigorous Christianization programme throughout the archdiocese in accordance with Tridentine requirements (Coleman, 2003, pp. 177–80). But the initiatives were met with resistance within some sectors of the local church and a further opportunity for instruction and integration was lost at a vital moment. The failure of Granadine clergy to accommodate the *morisco* and his reluctance to abandon his native culture increased tensions between the local church and its parishioners. A royal *pragmática* was published on 1 January 1567, prohibiting the practice of Moorish traditions within the kingdom of Granada. Measures included a ban on the use of Arabic and the wearing of silk garments, as well as the destruction of private and public baths, including those of the Alhambra. It amounted to a cultural annihilation. The anniversary of the surrender of Granada was deliberately chosen on which to announce the *pragmática*, thereby giving pointed offence. The age of co-operation between the two cultures had all but passed away. The conciliatory approach was about to be replaced by one of hard-line coercion.

The enforcement of the edict sparked off the outbreak of a violent uprising of Granadine *moriscos* in the Alpujarras mountains on Christmas Eve 1568 which lasted for two years and resulted in many atrocities on both sides. The king and senior ministers totally underestimated the local response to the imposition of the *pragmática*. It was naively assumed that forcing the *morisco* to abandon his ancient traditions would turn him into a loyal Christian subject, that one civilization could simply impose itself on another after centuries of cohabitation. The second revolt of the Alpujarras was also part of a wider jurisdictional struggle between the fourth Count of Tendilla, Captain General of Granada from 1543, who was regarded as being the protector of *morisco* peasants, and members of central government (represented via the legal tribunal known as the *Audiencia*), determined to impose their own administrative authority on the kingdom via the edict. Following the quelling of the revolt, a policy of re-settlement was put into immediate effect. Over 80,000 of the rebels were rounded up in November 1570 and the majority despatched in convoy to major cities in southern Castile. Toledo, Córdoba and Albacete took at least half of the exiled community. The dispersal of the seditious Granadine *morisco* community, so it was envisaged, would solve the problem. In practice it merely served to exacerbate it. The contagion spread throughout Castile rather than being confined to its southernmost kingdom (Lynch, 1965, I, pp. 211–18). Over a decade after the redistribution of the offending *granadinos*, the Archbishop of Toledo, Gaspar de Quiroga, reported to the Council of State on the failure of *morisco* integration within his own archdiocese. He took as his evidence a statement produced by a commissioner of the Toledan tribunal. He spoke of the lax orthodoxy of the *morisco* community in scathing terms:

> Diabolical unbelievers, they never go to mass, never accompany the Holy Sacrament through the streets, only go to confession for fear of sanctions against them. They marry amongst themselves, hide their children to avoid having them baptized, and when they do baptize them take the first passers-by on the church steps as godparents. Extreme unction is never requested except for those who are practically dead and unable to receive it. And since the

people responsible for supervising and educating these unbelievers do very little supervision or education, the latter do as
they please. (Braudel, 1976, II, p. 793)

This last remark reflects on the real root of the problem: almost a
hundred years after the Moors had been forced into Christian
baptism, the Primate of Spain was forced to acknowledge that
the evangelization programme had never made any significant
progress. His Church had effectively failed in its mission. The
morisco was still the Moor of old.

1570–1600: The End of Tolerance in Aragón

Following the crushing of the second Alpujarras revolt in 1570
and the ending of the 40-year moratorium on inquisitorial prosecutions, the focus of concern shifted to Spain's eastern provinces. There were some 135,000 *moriscos* in Valencia and around
half this number in Aragón, making up a third and a fifth
respectively of the local population in each region. In both
areas the New Christian community was multiplying fast. A 70
per cent growth rate was recorded in the kingdom of Valencia
between 1565 and 1609. The anticipation was that they might
soon outnumber the Old Christian population, which registered
a 45 per cent increase in the region over the same period (Lynch,
1969, II, pp. 44–5). The *moriscos* of the eastern kingdoms had
not suffered the same level of cultural repression as their co-
religionists in Granada. They lived in their own Moorish enclave,
resisting pressure to integrate into Christian society. Their most
committed defenders were their noble overlords who valued their
cheap labour force. Here the old Castilian proverb 'the more
Moors, the more profit' certainly rang true. At the same time,
there were those who were becoming increasingly intolerant of
their defiance. The tribunals of Valencia and Zaragoza stepped
up their prosecution of *moriscos* during the 1580s. Almost 2,500
were brought to trial in Valencia between 1566 and 1614 and
2,371 in Zaragoza over the same period (Contreras and
Henningsen, 1986, p. 118). These persecutions heightened political tensions between Old and New Christians in the eastern

kingdoms. By the end of the sixteenth century the *moriscos* in the east were regarded as a serious potential security risk. It was feared that the Aragonese were in collusion with the French Huguenots and that those of Valencia were seeking aid from their Ottoman allies.

Against this background, a meeting of Valencian bishops took place in 1573, under the chairmanship of Archbishop Juan de Ribera (1568–1611), to discuss ways of better instructing and integrating their *morisco* flock into the full body of the local church. A scheme was discussed to establish 22 new parishes in areas of high *morisco* settlement. Ribera, who had gained a reputation for his generous support of pastoral work in the archdiocese, promised to contribute 3,000 ducats per year to the project. The *plan parroquial* (parish regeneration programme) received papal approval in 1576 but a lack of funds and enthusiasm amongst the local clergy meant that the proposals made little headway in the decade that followed (Casey, 1999, p. 226). During the early 1580s, the idea of banishing all *moriscos* from Spain began to be mooted in ecclesiastical and political circles. Although agreed upon in principle, it took another two decades, marked by continued attempts to find a compromise solution, to put the expulsion order into effect. A *junta* of senior clergy met in Valencia in 1587 at the insistence of the Crown to discuss new initiatives. One of its members, Martín de Salvatierra, Bishop of Segorbe (1583–91), maintained that every effort had been made to accommodate the *moriscos* but they had failed to comply. They were, in his opinion, incorrigible enemies of the Catholic faith. The only option left was expulsion. Ribera himself was likely to have been of the same opinion but continued to support the official programme of evangelization and extension of the parochial infrastructure (Domínguez Ortiz and Vincent, 1978, pp. 71–2).

In 1597 an edict of grace was published by Pope Clement VIII by which Valencian *moriscos* were encouraged to abjure their errors and enter fully into the Catholic Church. As he ended his visit to Valencia in May 1599, Philip III instructed Ribera to press ahead with the publication of a catechism for the newly converted and to intensify the preaching mission. A report sent to the king in August 1601 by Valencian inquisitors confirmed that during the eighteen months of the edict, only thirteen people had come forward to confess their sins, some with dubious sincerity. By the end of 1601 the Archbishop could not contain his frustrations any longer. In a letter to the king he insisted on the obstinacy of the *moriscos* and the danger they represented. In January 1602 he wrote again to Philip, vigorously insisting on the need for expulsion or risk losing Spain to 'heretics and traitors'. The matter was now referred to the Council of State (Domínguez Ortiz and Vincent, 1978, pp. 159–67).

1600–1609: The Route to Expulsion

There was no unanimous call to expel the *moriscos* at this stage, from within either government, the Cortes or the Church. The Council of Inquisition was not formally consulted in the adoption of the final resolution. Divisions of opinion and of conscience continued to obstruct the decision-making process, just as they had done the attempted programme of assimilation. The Council of State came close to agreement in 1602 but the Duke of Lerma and the king's confessor, Fray Gaspar de Córdoba, were not yet convinced. Those who favoured expulsion – men motivated by the political threat rather than the religious one – were still in the minority. Ecclesiastical opinion in general did not support the harsh stand made by Ribera. The Bishop of Segorbe, Feliciano de Figueroa, reported in 1601 and again in 1604 of his success in bringing the faith to his *morisco* flock. Cardinal Fernando Niño de Guevara as Inquisitor General (1599–1602) refused to allow a global condemnation of the *moriscos*. In his treatise of 1606, the chronicler Pedro de Valencia, as well as acknowledging the failings of the *moriscos* themselves, also put forward a series of rational solutions to the *morisco* problem. He strongly advised against the use of religion for political purposes. Instead he proposed that measures should be taken to integrate the *morisco* into Christian society on equal terms and to provide for their proper conversion and assimilation into the Catholic Church. Valencia's paper bore witness to the endurance of a tolerant, dispassionate current of thought in Spanish society, humanist in spirit, free from the prejudice and fanaticism that prevailed in religious circles on the eve of the expulsion:

> In order to aid their conversion, the *Moriscos* must be compelled
> to abandon their Moorish dress and customs. But this must be
> done in a gentle rather than forceful way, without any interven-
> tion from the Holy Inquisition, for when they are subject to harsh
> tactics, they become rebellious and corrective measures, such as
> beatings and confiscations of goods, are interpreted as acts of
> vengeance by the enemy. As a result, they dig their heels in
> further. (Jones, 1997, pp. 168–9)

A *junta* of three senior ministers (including the newly
appointed royal confessor Fray Jerónimo de Javierre, General
of the Dominican Order), who met in January and October 1607,
recommended the renewal of Christian teaching and missionary
work under the direction of committed priests and members of
the religious orders. But within a matter of months, a majority
decision was taken at a session of the Council of State (convened
on 30 January 1608) to support a policy of expulsion. This
dramatic reversal of intent may have been prompted by the
Duke of Lerma, persuaded by Archbishop Ribera, who seized
an opportune moment to reap maximum personal and political
advantage. The shock discovery of a planned *morisco* uprising
in Valencia, scheduled for Maundy Thursday 1605, involving
French and Algerian participation, may also have forced events.
However, the decision taken by the Council was not publicly
disclosed at this juncture. Indeed, there was still considerable
division of opinion on the issue. In November 1608 a group of
leading Valencian theologians met to consider the *morisco* problem at the insistence of Pope Paul V, who continued to advocate
a conciliatory solution. The Bishops of Orihuela, Tortosa and
Segorbe declared themselves in favour of the continuation of the
Christianization programme (providing evidence of success
within their own dioceses), a recommendation quite at odds
with that which had already been taken in Madrid.

The formal decision to expel the *moriscos* was taken by the
Council of State on 4 April 1609 and approved by Philip III five
days later, the same day on which Spain signed a twelve-year
truce with the Dutch rebels. Public attention was thus diverted
from the humiliating withdrawal of troops from the Netherlands
while Spanish garrisons reassembled to aid in the deportation

process. The first expulsion order was published in Valencia on 22 September 1609 (Domínguez Ortiz and Vincent, 1978, pp. 177–80). Five days later, Archbishop Ribera delivered a sermon in which he justified the banishment of the *moriscos* on religious grounds. He referred to the dishonour suffered by true Christians through their forced co-existence with infidels and the need to placate God for their having tolerated non-believers for so long. The old crusading militancy of the Spanish Church, rooted in the Reconquest, was thus dramatically rekindled in order to win over public opinion. Lerma skilfully avoided confrontation with his fellow Valencian overlords by allowing them to retain the personal property and real estate (*bienes muebles y raíces*) of their *morisco* tenants. Between September 1609 and January 1610, an estimated total of 135,000 *moriscos* were deported from the kingdom of Valencia – potentially the most dangerous area of *morisco* habitation. They were followed by their co-religionists from Castile, Extremadura, La Mancha, Andalusia, Murcia, Catalonia and Aragón. By the end of March 1611, the main part of the operation was complete with pockets of resistance having been successfully crushed. A total of nearly 300,000 *moriscos* had been forced to leave Spain for France and North Africa. To these must be added the 10,000–12,000 identified by Domínguez Ortiz and Vincent as having lost their lives in rebellions en route to their places of departure (see table 4.1). The expulsion marked the ultimate failure of Spanish society to accept the cultural diversity of the *mudéjar* community and to properly assimilate the *morisco* into the Christian faith. The Inquisition had proved itself ineffective in their regard. By presenting the event as a great moral victory for Catholicism, the political calculations inherent in the dispersal were disguised, as was the conflict of attitudes within both lay and ecclesiastical circles that lay behind it.

1609–1614: The Aftermath

The 23 per cent depletion of the population in the kingdom of Valencia prompted a severe agricultural and economic recession in the region, compounding the demographic and agrarian crisis

Table 4.1   The expulsion of the *moriscos* by region, 1609–11

	Number of expulsions	% loss
Kingdom of Castile		
(a) *Central regions*		
Old and New Castile,		
La Mancha, Extremadura	45,000	0.9
(b) *Southern regions*		
Murcia, Canaries, Granada,		
Andalusia	50,000	2.7
Crown of Aragón		
Aragón	61,000	15.2
Catalonia	5,000	1.0
Valencia	135,000	23.0
Total losses	296,000	3.7

Source: Lapeyre, 1986, p. 252

afflicting neighbouring Castile. As early as May 1610, the *Audiencia* (High Court of Appeal) of Valencia was lamenting the scarcity of hard-working labourers caused by the expulsion of the *moriscos*. Landowners, dependent on *morisco* rents, failed to make their mortgage payments to their creditors, who included ecclesiastical communities. In February 1612, the Court historian Cabrera de Córdoba reported that the rental income of the Archbishop of Valencia had declined from 70,000 to 50,000 ducats per annum following the depopulation of the area. The economic stability of the Inquisition in the eastern kingdoms was also severely affected by the expulsion. The Valencian tribunal suffered a 42.7 per cent loss of income from taxes and subsidies payable by the *morisco* population. Its counterpart in Zaragoza had its income reduced by over 48 per cent (Kamen, 1985, p. 112). Both tribunals sought financial compensation from the government for their loss of revenue. The exodus of the *moriscos* thus deprived agriculture of skilled manpower and specialist farming methods and the economy of sizeable returns. This consequence had clearly been envisaged, for the decree exempted 6 per cent of all families from expulsion 'so that dwellings, sugar mills, rice harvests, and irrigation systems may be preserved, and so they may give instruction to new settlers', but few took advantage

(Lynch, 1969, II, p. 46; Domínguez Ortiz and Vincent, 1978, p. 180). Although the Crown made considerable ready profit from the exercise, via seizures of goods and property, the monies were soon dissipated. The famous *consulta* of the Council of Castile of 1619 did not list the Moorish expulsion among the numerous causes of Spain's economic decline, nor did contemporary commentators of the phenomenon (known as the *arbitristas*) raise it as an issue. But there is no doubt that it had a serious impact, particularly in the eastern kingdoms. Of the 453 *morisco* villages of Valencia, abandoned in 1609, over 200 remained uninhabited in 1638 (Domínguez Ortiz and Vincent, 1978, p. 219).

Some managed to avoid enforced exile and remain in their adoptive land. The Inquisition, that had obediently accepted the expulsion, curiously and paradoxically became a refuge for those *moriscos* who resisted the order and, upon interrogation, instantly vowed to accept Christianity. In January 1610 the tribunal of Valencia reported that:

> Some Moriscos have intended to or intend to remain in this kingdom and not to embark with the others, and those of whom we have up to now known to have this intention amount to about a dozen; we have been hearing their spontaneous confessions, wherein they declare to have been Moors, and firmly profess to convert and live and die as Christians; and we understand that there are some others who have the same intention, and because it seems to us that we are obligated to hear and receive them, we are doing so although the possibility exists that some would merely pretend to have these intentions of conversion. (García-Cárcel, 1987, p. 83)

Ecclesiastical opinion remained divided. In January 1610 the Archbishop of Seville made a plea for clemency on behalf of those *moriscos* remaining in the city of Granada who were respected members of the local church (Domínguez Ortiz and Vincent, 1978, pp. 281–2). In October 1611 Philip III signed an expulsion order on all the 2,500 inhabitants of the community of the Valle del Ricote in Murcia. Many appealed against this decision, including Fray Juan de Pereda (emissary of the royal confessor), who wrote an account in April 1612 of the different sorts of *moriscos* who lived in the kingdom, insisting on the Christianity of those of the Valle del Ricote. They were in the habit of drinking wine and eating pork. Those under 40 did not speak or understand Arabic:

> And it is rare to find a witness that does not confirm that none dresses in Moorish fashion, that they usually drink wine and the majority eats bacon. In this they differ greatly from the *moriscos* of Granada and Valencia. [. . .] The difference is also manifest in their language, for those who are under 40 do not speak Arabic nor do they understand it. Lastly, all witnesses confirm that in all things pertaining to Christianity the *moriscos* [of the Valle del Ricote] are like saints compared to their compatriots in Granada, Valencia and Aragón. [. . .] Those people who speak most earnestly about the sincerity of their faith are confessors and those who have had individual contact with them. (Lapeyre, 1986, Appendix xvi) [translated by HR]

But hardliners on the Council of State refused to be moved, alleging the demonstration of their Christianity to be nothing but a superficial act of pretence. Some had apparently joined religious orders to avoid enforced exile. The expulsion went ahead in October 1613. A total of 6,000–7,000 *moriscos* were forced out of their Murcian homeland. But such was their devotion to their roots that many returned illegally from exile. Although subjected to punishment they continued to defy the authorities who gave up their chase in 1626 and allowed them to settle once again in *their* kingdom. Cervantes, via the character of Ricote in Part II of *Don Quijote*, expressed his own underlying sympathy (and possibly that of a wider public) for the banished *morisco* by making him the mouthpiece of the sadness and bitterness of a condemned community and race. 'To us', claimed Ricote, 'it [exile] was the most terrible [punishment] that could be inflicted. Wherever we are we weep for Spain; for, after all, we were born here and this is our native country. Nowhere do we find the reception our misery requires', he lamented.

By 1614, the Moorish enemy, the false convert, who had refused to abandon the traditions of his mother culture, who was reported to be in collusion with Spain's foreign enemies and who had reaped profit at the expense of the Spaniard by his hard

work and thriftiness, had been excluded. The religious motivation for the expulsion, compounded by the political threat,
concealed a long-standing animosity on the part of the Christian
towards the Moorish convert, partly rooted in the successful
survival of the alien culture. As Fernand Braudel has acknowledged: 'The *Morisco* after one, two or even three centuries,
remained still the Moor of old, with his Moorish dress, tongue,
cloistered house and Moorish baths. He had retained them all.
He had refused to accept western civilization and this was his
fundamental crime' (Braudel, 1976, II, p. 796). The expulsion of
the *moriscos* both symbolized the bitterness felt by a defeated
nation and was at the same time symptomatic of the internal
dilemma of a society ill at ease with its past and uncertain about
its future. The doubts lingered. Antonio de Sotomayor, the royal
confessor, remarked in 1633: 'It is a very short time since the
Moriscos were expelled, an action that did much harm to these
kingdoms, that it would be a good idea to have them back, if they
could be persuaded to accept our Holy Faith' (Elliott, 1983,
p. 308). The *morisco* may have been forced out of Spain but his
cultural heritage would live on.

5 The Inquisition and Protestantism

During the opening decades of the sixteenth century the religious foundations of early modern Europe underwent a dramatic transformation. The rise of Lutheranism in Germany in the 1520s prompted a movement of radical reform within the western Church, referred to by modern historians as 'the Reformation'. It resulted in the formation of the Protestant Church, which promoted a liberal approach to Christian belief and worship, set to rival the Church of Rome, which in turn responded by reinforcing the orthodox principles of its foundation. Spain, despite its firm commitment to Catholicism, was not unaffected by these events. Although the reforms initiated under Ferdinand and Isabella in the late fifteenth century, and taken forward by Francisco Jiménez de Cisneros as Archbishop of Toledo (1495–1517), had served to deepen popular piety and strengthen ecclesiastical discipline within the Spanish Church, they left untouched its structure and its doctrines: the main foci of reformist criticism. Indeed, Cisneros' promotion of devotional literature in the vernacular may well have contributed to producing a climate favourable to the reception of new trends in religious thought penetrating northern Europe. The invention of the printing press, the growth in interest in biblical scholarship and links with Europe via the imperial inheritance of Charles V, all served to encourage the spread of evangelical views in Spain during the first half of the sixteenth century. Nevertheless, the emergence of the Reformed Church led to the hardening of traditional, conservative attitudes within ecclesiastical circles. Spain, unlike its northern neighbours, had the machinery of the Inquisition at its disposal, which it had already brought to bear effectively on backsliding Jews and which it was now prepared to use to purge Spain of any potentially subversive infiltrations of belief. From the late 1520s the Inquisition deliberately set about associating innovative trends in religious and intellectual life with Lutheran heresy, however far removed they were in actual fact from such a definition. In addition, by actively seeking new sources of contagion, it substantially expanded its power base that had been considerably diminished since the end of the period of intense anti-*converso* persecutions.

Illuminism and Humanism under Attack

The Inquisition's attack on the Illuminist movement was the first phase in this process. The Illuminists or *Alumbrados* were a small elite group of spiritual devotees, based in New Castile, inspired by their reading of devotional literature which advocated the virtues of private meditative prayer over formal ceremony as a means of attaining perfect union with God. The movement, which attracted New Christian followers, sheltered under the protection of members of the Castilian aristocracy and was inspired and supported by the Franciscans. Although its origins are obscure, it is unlikely to have owed anything directly to the northern reform movement. However, it was not long before it aroused the suspicions of the Inquisition. By encouraging a personalized faith, it was seen to share common ground with the dangerous currents of religious reform simultaneously penetrating Europe. In 1524 leading members of the original conventicle of Illuminists, who met in Guadalajara, including the *beata* (female devotee) Isabel de la Cruz and the lay preacher Pedro Ruiz de Alcaraz – both of *converso* origin – were arrested by the Inquisition of Toledo for disseminating a deviant form of spirituality. Other circles were later uncovered operating in and around Salamanca, Valladolid and Alcalá. In 1525 the Inquisition incorporated *alumbrado* heresy into the edict of faith.

EDICT OF FAITH INVITING PEOPLE TO IDENTIFY *ALUMBRADOS* IN THEIR MIDST, 1525 (ADAPTED)

If you know or have heard it said that any person has affirmed that mental prayer alone is divinely ordained and that it is of greater worth than vocal prayer; [...] and that it is not necessary to obey a prelate, priest or superior in so far as they demand acts which interfere with mental prayer and contemplation, and that nobody can be virtuous unless they undertake such practices; and they speak words disparaging of the sacrament of marriage; and that no one can grasp the secret of virtue unless they become disciples of the masters who teach the said pernicious doctrine; and that no one can be saved without the prayers which the said masters teach [...] and that certain experiences of stirring, shivering, pain and fainting are signs of God's love and that through such love they know they are in a state of grace with the Holy Spirit [...] and that when one arrives at a certain level of perfection, one can perceive in this life the divine essence and mysteries of the Trinity; and that the Holy Spirit directly rules those who live in this way and that one only has to follow its inspiration to know how one should behave ... [may they declare it].

Source: Jiménez Monteserín, 1980, pp. 516–19 [translated by HR]

Numerically the trials of *alumbrados* were of little significance in the history of the Spanish Inquisition. Inquisitors found it difficult to categorize this new form of heresy. Sentences were light and some trials were suspended through lack of evidence. The *alumbrado* was seen as a kind of 'hybrid heretic', tenuously linked to the old, virtually contained, heresy of Judaism and the new, potentially dangerous, threat of Lutheranism. As the reform movement in northern Europe gathered momentum, *alumbradismo* became a useful charge to level against any form of innovation in spiritual and intellectual life, including Erasmianism and later Protestantism (Kinder, 1992, pp. 218–21; Hamilton, 1992, pp. 25–42, 51–63).

During the 1520s, the writings of the distinguished Dutch humanist scholar Desiderius Erasmus (*c*.1466–1536) began to influence Spanish religious and intellectual life as a result of his following at the imperial court of Charles V, king of Spain (1516–56) and Holy Roman Emperor (1519–58). Erasmus supported the dissemination of a new form of religious culture, known as Christian Humanism. The humanist tradition, in which piety and learning were intimately linked, evolved from ideas promoted in northern Europe during the Renaissance. It encouraged the wider interpretation of biblical scholarship via its classical routes, leading to a revitalized expression of belief. Erasmus outlined these notions in his *Enchiridion Militis Christiani* (Handbook of a Christian Soldier), first published in 1503. In it he criticized paganism, superstition and immorality in the Church (notably within the monastic orders). He called for a reformed, less ritualistic, more tolerant faith that accommodated intellectual freedom, private prayer and meditation. Erasmus hoped that peace and spiritual reconciliation might be achieved between traditionalists and reformists within the Christian Church, a notion that accorded with Charles V's vision of himself as a universal Emperor ruling over a universal Church.

Erasmianism was a movement with political, social and religious overtones that responded to many of the preoccupations of the early modern age. It soon acquired an enthusiastic following in Spain, especially among those religious and courtiers who had travelled with the imperial court through northern Europe. The two most senior ecclesiastics in Spain, Alonso Manrique de Lara, the Inquisitor General (1523–38), and Alonso de Fonseca, Archbishop of Toledo (1523–34), were both ardent supporters of Erasmus's views. Outside immediate court circles, many Erasmian sympathizers were characterized by their New Christian ancestry, their Illuminist background and their association with the Complutensian University of Alcalá. During the 1520s, under the patronage of Archbishop Jiménez de Cisneros, the university became a thriving centre for theological debate and inquiry. In 1522 (the same year in which Luther's New Testament appeared in print), the famous Polyglot Bible was published by the Complutensian press. Many distinguished scholars (including Erasmus) were invited to take part in the project, designed to 'improve the dissemination of the word of God'. Three years later, the writings of Erasmus began to roll off the Alcalá printing press and in 1526, a Castilian version of the *Enchiridion*, translated by the canon of Palencia, Alonso Fernández de Madrid, appeared in print for the first time. Such was its appeal that it immediately sold out. Eight editions were printed in Spain over the next four years. The book was reported to be so popular that it was read 'in the cities, in the churches, in the convents, even in the inns and highways [...] by people of every sort' (Bataillon, 1966, p. 280). The propagation of Erasmian humanism through the printed word injected new life into the Illuminist movement, with which it shared much common ground. But the success of Erasmianism in Spain was to be short-lived. Within a year of the publication of the *Enchiridion* in Castilian, attempts were under way to undermine Erasmus, his supporters and the whole spirit of regeneration with which he was associated.

In June 1527, an ecclesiastical Congregation met at Valladolid. Those assembled were divided in their views on Erasmus. The anti-Erasmian faction was led by Franciscans and Dominicans, profoundly suspicious of his anti-monastic views, as summed up in his famous dictum – *monochatus non est pietas* – by which Erasmus implied that membership of the religious orders did not necessarily mean being of higher worth than those who lived a non-celibate life, nor did it guarantee an adherence to Christian values. They were supported by leading theologians from Salamanca, who disapproved of his attack on scholastic theology. They exposed the 'twenty-two errors of Erasmus' before those gathered in Congregation. The pro-Erasmian faction, led by humanist scholars from Alcalá and the movement's partisans within the ecclesiastical hierarchy, rejected these accusations. The divergence of views expressed in the Valladolid debate equated with the emerging divisions within the western Church, with the pro-Erasmians advocating a reformist approach to Christian belief and the anti-Erasmians a traditional, orthodox one. When Archbishop Manrique brought the proceedings of the Congregation to a sudden end, two months after its opening, the issues remained as contentious as ever (Bataillon, 1966, pp. 248–78).

Three events in 1529 prompted a dramatic downturn in the fortunes of Erasmus and his followers in Spain. In July, Charles left Spain for Italy, taking with him the leading Erasmians from his household. Shortly afterwards, Inquisitor General Manrique fell from favour and was forced to retire to his Archdiocese of Seville. In the same year, Francisca Hernández, the leader of the

Valladolid Illuminist circle, was arrested and went on to maliciously denounce fellow devotees to the Inquisition as Erasmian humanists of Lutheran orientation. The position of Erasmians was reduced to that of a vulnerable minority of intellectuals, deprived of support and suspected of unorthodox leanings. The strengthened campaign against Erasmus, launched in the early 1530s, represented a tactical display of force by the conservatives who dominated the Inquisition, now enjoying a much freer hand in Spain in the absence of the Emperor and his foreign advisers. The Inquisition's moves to eradicate Erasmianism also have to be set against the background of emerging religious turmoil within Europe. In 1529, a number of German princes signed a 'Protestation', pledging their support for what henceforth became known as the Protestant Church. Two years later, they banded together against Imperial religious policies by forming the League of Schmalkalden. The Holy Roman Empire was set to become a divided land of two churches, one Protestant and the other Catholic, and susceptible to the growth of extreme sects within. The Inquisition responded by attempting to discredit any potentially damaging currents of belief that it suspected might be associated with the heresy spreading through northern Europe, and therefore capable of destabilizing the authority of the Catholic state. It chose as its first victim one of the most highly acclaimed humanist scholars in Spain.

In June 1533, Juan de Vergara was arrested and imprisoned by the Holy Office, charged with suborning the work of the Inquisition and of being a Lutheran, Illuminist and Erasmian sympathizer. Vergara, who had collaborated in the Polyglot Bible project at Alcalá, first met Erasmus in 1520 while on an official visit to the Flemish court and established a firm friendship with him. Throughout the decade that followed, Vergara distinguished himself as one of the leading exponents of Erasmian reform in Spain, while at the same time occupying the positions of court chaplain to Charles V (1522) and private secretary to the Spanish Primate, Alonso de Fonseca (1523). Vergara was accused of 'knowing, teaching and believing the errors of those called *alumbrados* which almost coincide with the said Lutheran errors' (Hamilton, 1992, p. 85). He vigorously defended himself at his trial, refusing to accept that his friendship with Erasmus constituted a crime or that he had any sympathy with Lutheran doctrine. The inquisitors' verdict was announced, significantly, following the death in February 1534 of Vergara's patron, Fonseca. Vergara was forced to abjure his errors *de vehementi* in an *auto de fe*, held in the Plaza de Zocodover in Toledo on 21 December 1535. He was sentenced to a year of monastic seclusion (later transmuted into confinement within the cathedral grounds) and forced to pay a fine of 1,500 ducats. When Vergara was released in February 1537, almost four years after his original arrest, he resumed his position as a canon of Toledo with the support and respect of the church community (Bataillon, 1966, pp. 438–70).

Vergara was a member of the intellectual and ecclesiastical elite, stimulated by his contact with new ideas emanating from northern Europe. He embraced a flexible religious culture, one that was perhaps more widespread among Spanish scholars than has hitherto been acknowledged. He was far removed from being a subversive figure within the Catholic Church as the Holy Office sought to label him. Other prominent Erasmians, such as the *converso* theologian and commentator on the Holy Scriptures, Juan de Valdés, and the chancellor of the University of Alcalá, Pedro de Lerma, chose to leave Spain rather than fall victims to the campaign to discredit their tolerant tradition. By the mid-1530s, the Inquisition, under heavy Dominican influence, had effectively enforced silence on humanist scholarship as part of its campaign to turn Spain into a fortress against heresy. It now turned its attention to hounding some of the great Catholic reformers of the period who contributed to Spain's religious revival in the first half of the sixteenth century – Juan de Ávila, Ignatius Loyola and Teresa de Jesús – all of whom, significantly, were later recognized as saints.

Innovation in Religious Life Condemned

Juan de Ávila made a major contribution to the revitalization of religious life in early sixteenth-century Spain in his role as a popular preacher, writer and clerical reformer. During his formative years as a student at the University of Alcalá he had become familiar with the writings of Erasmus. In 1526, with the support of Archbishop Manrique, Ávila began his career as a priest in southern Spain, where he appealed directly to the spiritual needs of the people. Such was the strength of his inspiration that he became known as 'The Apostle of Andalusia'. He travelled through the region preaching, hearing confessions, organizing aid for the poor and promoting religious education. He called for a renewed sense of vocation amongst the priesthood and criticized the system of hereditary appointments to lesser clerical offices which enabled young men to become priests simply on account of their family lineage. In 1531, at the height of his success, Juan de Ávila was arrested for publicly suggesting that 'it was better to give alms than to found chaplaincies' and that '[in Andalusia] there is [an] insufficient number of masses and extreme misery amongst the poor' (Bilinkoff, 1989, pp. 80–7). His theology, with its emphasis on works of charity and acts of simple faith, attracted many, like their 'Apostle', who were of New Christian descent. In the prevailing climate of spiritual unease, Ávila's reformist ideals and his methods of devotion, which had much in common with those advocated by Illuminist and Humanist thinkers, set a dangerous challenge to orthodoxy in the eyes of the ecclesiastical authorities. Above all, it was the power and success of Ávila's apostolate that prompted the mistrust (and jealousy) of academics and theologians within the Church, especially those of the Dominican Order, widely represented on the Inquisition, who refused to accept any other than the traditional route to God, with its emphasis on doctrine, ceremony and public prayer.

Such was the flimsiness of the inquisitorial case brought against Ávila that within two years he was cleared of all charges and released from imprisonment. He returned to take up his preaching role in Andalusia, founding a college in 1537 for the training of priests (the *Colegio Eclesiástico de San Cecilio*) that was later to provide a model for the Tridentine seminary. He also developed around him a sacerdotal school dominated by New Christians that engaged in apostolic missions. While in prison Juan de Ávila had begun to write his most celebrated work – a commentary on Psalm 44, the *Audi, filia*, in which he warned his readers of the dangers of Illuminism – the very 'crime' of which he had been accused. The text, which first appeared in manuscript form in 1556, was seized upon by the heavy hand of Inquisitor General Valdés in 1559 for its heretical content and withdrawn from circulation. A man of highly suspect spirituality in the eyes of the Inquisition, Ávila nevertheless continued to influence the course of Spanish Catholicism into the Counter-Reformation period. He wrote a catechism in the vernacular (*Doctrina cristiana*), which transformed the religious education of the laity, and prepared a written outline of his proposals for clerical reform which the Archbishop of Granada, Don Pedro Guerrero, incorporated into his address to the second session of the Council of Trent (Coleman, 2003, pp. 137–44). Five years after Juan de Ávila's death in 1574, under the more accommodating regime of Inquisitor General Gaspar de Quiroga, a revised edition of the *Audi, filia* was published in Toledo. The influence of Juan de Ávila would live on.

Juan de Ávila's methods of prayer and meditation, as well as his reforming zeal, won him a number of keen disciples, among them Ignatius Loyola, the founder of the Jesuits. In 1522, profoundly influenced by his reading of devotional literature, Loyola chose to withdraw from secular life and adopt a semi-monastic existence of extreme austerity. In pursuit of spiritual guidance, he set out on a pilgrimage to Jerusalem and the Holy Land. He had begun the first draft of his *Spiritual Exercises* – a practical guide for the direction of souls, which set out a month-long programme of intensive self-examination, meditation and prayer, leading to a strengthening of the practitioner's will and his total submission to the cause of Catholicism. The *Exercises* were a unique statement of spiritual commitment. Not only did they become the fundamental manual of Jesuit instruction but furthermore, while pre-dating Trent, they embodied the essential elements of its doctrine. Shortly after his return to Spain in 1524 Loyola took up the study of theology at Alcalá and soon became immersed in Erasmian circles. The intense activities of his prayer groups set the Inquisition on his trail. He was arrested in April 1526 as a suspected Illuminist. No sooner had he been absolved (and banned from preaching for three years) than he found himself in a similar confrontation, this time with church authorities in Salamanca. To avoid further persecution he left Spain for

France in 1527, never to return to his homeland. While studying
at the Sorbonne he assembled around him nine 'brothers', the
founder members of the Society of Jesus, four of whom were
Spaniards. In August 1534 at Montmartre they committed themselves to their apostolic ideal. The Society, born out of the drive
for spiritual renewal within the Catholic Church as it adapted
itself to the challenges of the early modern era, was formally
established by a papal bull of September 1540. It was set to
become the international cornerstone of the Counter-Reformation's world-wide teaching mission.

   But controversy continued to surround the Society in Spain.
In the early 1550s Melchor Cano, a Dominican professor of
theology at Salamanca and a fierce opponent of innovative
forces within the Church, claimed that the Jesuits 'would corrupt
the simplicity and Christianity of Spain' (Hamilton, 1992, p. 97).
The *Spiritual Exercises*, so he maintained, shared much in common with Illuminism, by promoting an interior form of religious
experience rather than one that adhered to the formal elements
of orthodox tradition. There was also a racial element to the
attack. Although Loyola himself was of Old Christian ancestry,
the Society remained open to men of *converso* origin until 1592,
attracting among others some of the original disciples of Juan de
Ávila, thereby raising suspicions of Jewish subversion within its
ranks. Loyola continued to be hounded by his enemies beyond
his death in 1556. Along with so many works of mystical inspiration, the *Spiritual Exercises* fell victim to inquisitorial censorship in the 1559 Index of prohibited books. Traditionalists within
the Spanish Church regarded the Jesuits as rivals who owed
allegiance to the papacy before the Crown and whose commitment went far beyond Spain. Despite these setbacks, the Jesuits
remained among the most vociferous opponents of the stifling of
innovative forms of spiritual expression in sixteenth-century
Spain and key agents in the application of religious reform at
local and diocesan level.

   Similar suspicions surrounded the founder of the Discalced
Carmelite movement, Teresa de Ahumada y Cespeda, canonized
in 1622 as Santa Teresa de Jesús, known to us as Teresa of Ávila.
Teresa de Ávila was a product of the vibrant expression of
spirituality that characterized Spanish religious life during the

opening decades of the sixteenth century. Her spiritual calling had begun in the 1530s, at the time when Juan de Ávila and Ignatius Loyola were establishing their movements. As a young Carmelite nun, she too became deeply influenced by the reading of devotional literature (especially Francisco de Osuna's *Spiritual ABC*) which described the inner spiritual life, oriented towards the quiet reception of God through mental prayer. In the 1540s she was drawn, through a series of divine revelations, to renounce the things of this world and seek instead a humble life of prayer and devotion. One of Teresa's closest spiritual mentors was Juan de Ávila, whom she described as 'a man deeply versed in everything relating to prayer'. Inspired by his example, as well as by that of other religious reformers (especially the austere spirituality of the founder of the Discalced Franciscans, Pedro of Alcántara), Teresa dedicated herself to religious reform. In 1561 she embarked upon her missionary role – to reform the lax rule of the Carmelites. Her aim was to replace the elitist principles which had governed entry to the Order for generations by those of poverty, humility, piety and obedience – characteristics of the primitive rule which had inspired the Carmelite movement's original foundation in the mid-thirteenth century. Furthermore, her objectives were in perfect accord with the proposals for monastic reform outlined by Catholic bishops and theologians at the Council of Trent. Following the inauguration of the first Discalced Carmelite convent (Saint Joseph's) in Ávila on 24 August 1562, Teresa set about a twenty-year period of radical reforming activity.

Teresa's mystical experiences, intimately described in her writings, coincided with a period of intense reaction on the part of the Church hierarchy against any form of innovative spiritual expression that was not subject to its direct control and therefore threatened to undermine its authority. In 1562, the year of the foundation of Saint Joseph's, Teresa finished writing her autobiography, *Libro de la Vida*, in which she recorded in simple, direct prose her own personal experiences of divine revelation, and gave instructions as to how others could follow the mystical way. Its publication, however, was deferred on account of the suspicions surrounding her meditative practices. As her writings fell under scrutiny she was denounced to the Inquisition and accused in 1575 of spreading superstition and of influencing the *alumbrado* community of Seville. Teresa's Jewish blood (inherited from her paternal grandfather – a wealthy New Christian merchant and tax farmer in Toledo) cast a further layer of suspicion on her person and her movement which, like the Jesuits, permitted the participation of *conversos*. With the support of Philip II and Inquisitor General Quiroga, the campaign against Teresa was dropped. A remarkable reappraisal of Spanish mysticism took place during the later sixteenth century as the Inquisition entered a less repressive phase of its history and Trent stimulated a revival of intense forms of pious devotion that had earlier been stifled in Spain. The deep spirituality that Teresa de Ávila espoused was now recognized as a fundamental aid to Catholic reform, rather than as a threat to it. In her commitment to strengthen orthodoxy through prayer, she personified the intense religiosity and contemplative spirit of Spanish Catholicism in the Counter-Reformation era. Her writings, collected and edited by Fray Luis de León, were finally approved for publication in 1588, six years after her death. Her elevation to sainthood in 1622 formally confirmed her exalted status within the Catholic Church (Eire, 1995, p. 502–10).

The Protestant Challenge, 1558–1559

The precautionary investigations made by the Holy Office during the first half of the sixteenth century into those intellectuals of suspect spiritual persuasion were followed in the 1550s by the launching of a vigorous attack on what was perceived to be an infiltration of Protestant influences into Spain. Before the Council of Trent met in its first session (1545–8) to redefine Catholic doctrine, there was still genuine ignorance and misunderstanding among Spaniards as to what actually constituted Protestantism. Until mid-century Luther's teachings had been read by only a small minority of intellectuals – erudite clergy and liberal-minded professors – who had access to trends in European thought but whose influence over religious belief in Spain was marginal. The principal definition of a Lutheran where inquisitors were concerned was somebody who made a passing reference in praise of a reformer or his ideas. In the majority of cases 'Lutheranism' amounted to nothing more than a careless religious statement rather than a calculated attack on the Catholic Church. The Inquisition made general use of the concept to denounce certain types of belief and non-orthodox practice, to reinforce social cohesion and to promote adherence to a regulated ideology (Contreras, 1987a, pp. 57–62).

Protestantism became identifiable via elements of speech or belief rather than by particular traits of behaviour, as was the case with *conversos* and *moriscos*. By the 1560s the Holy Office had reduced 'Lutheranism' to seven cardinal errors or doctrinal positions against which they determined the guilt of those accused. Protestants were people characterized by: (1) their denial of the existence of purgatory; (2) their opposition to the worship of saints and the Virgin Mary; (3) their ridicule of the authority of the Pope and his bulls; (4) their non-acceptance of clerical celibacy; (5) their refusal to confess with a priest; (6) their non-observance of fasting during holidays or during Lent; and (7) their denial of the real presence of Christ's body in the Eucharist. Only a few were found guilty of all seven errors, some of which overlapped with Jewish and Muslim heresies in their objections to Catholicism. In practice a huge gulf existed between 'dogmatic Lutheranism', that is a belief in the theology of Protestant reformers, and the cases of 'sociological Lutheranism' that came before the tribunals of the Inquisition and which shared much in common with other forms of religious dissent (Dedieu, 1979c, pp. 269–91).

EDICT OF FAITH INVITING PEOPLE TO IDENTIFY LUTHERANS WITHIN THEIR MIDST (ADAPTED)

Item, if you know that any person or persons have said, held or believed that the false and perverted sect of Martin Luther and his followers is sound, or have believed in or approved of their opinions, saying that it is not necessary to make confession to the priest, that it is sufficient to confess before God alone and that neither the Pope nor priests have power to give absolution for sins; that the consecrated Host is not the real body of Our Lord Jesus Christ; that it is not necessary to pray to the Saints and there should be no images in the churches; that there is no purgatory, and there is no need to pray for the dead; that good works are not necessary, and that faith and baptism suffice for salvation through the Passion of Our Lord Jesus Christ who paid for all; that anyone can confess and give Holy Communion to one another; and that the Pope has no power with regard to indulgences, pardons or bulls, and that priests, monks and nuns may marry; and that the Religious Orders should be abolished; and that the ceremonies of the church should be done away with and that only Sundays should be kept holy; that it is not a sin to eat meat on Fridays or in Lent or on days of abstinence because there is no day on which it is forbidden for them and that the state of matrimony is better (in the sight of God) than the celibate state of the clergy...[may they declare it].

Source: Jiménez Monteserín, 1980, pp. 514–16 [translated by HR]

Of the alleged 105 'Lutherans' brought before the Spanish Inquisition prior to 1558, 66 were foreigners and 39 natives. Cases of Protestant heresy were dealt with predominantly by frontier tribunals – those of Logroño, Zaragoza and Barcelona in the north and Seville in the south – situated in peripheral areas 'open' to the passage of trade and ideas. From 1547 to 1599, 60 per cent of those 'Protestants' brought before the Aragonese tribunals were of French origin, although the majority had had no contact with organized Lutheran or Calvinist churches in France. In practice, the Reformation stood little real chance of establishing itself in Spain – the only country in western Europe which possessed a powerful institution whose designated purpose was to preserve its orthodoxy. Nevertheless, the Spanish kingdoms did not remain totally impervious to the dramatic effects of the spread of the Reformed Church through northern Europe. When it was announced in the late 1550s that Lutheran heresy had apparently penetrated Spain's religious defences and established a native root in two of its major cities – Seville and Valladolid – it threatened to destabilize the country's image at home and abroad as the guardian of the faith.

In May 1558 a Protestant 'cell' was uncovered in Valladolid, where the royal Court was in residence. What made the discovery most alarming was the high social and intellectual standing of those involved. Almost simultaneously, the existence of a parallel group of Protestant sympathizers within the ecclesiastical community of Seville was formally announced. The detection of heresy within senior religious and courtly circles sent a wave of panic through the political establishment. The scandal unleashed by the Protestant discoveries threatened the position of the Inquisitor General, Fernando de Valdés (1547–65), but he skilfully seized the opportunity to strengthen rather than undermine his power base at the Holy Office (Lea, 1922, III, pp. 426–36; González Novalín, 1968, I, pp. 290–323; Rodríguez Salgado, 1988, pp. 215–19). In September 1558, given the context within which Protestant activity was being uncovered, Valdés secured the approval of Paul IV to extend the investigative powers of the Inquisition beyond the secular reaches of society to include members of the Church hierarchy (Lea, 1922, III, p. 556). This was a crucial papal concession and a turning point in the history of the Inquisition. Armed with its increased authority, the Holy Office embarked on a new, aggressive and highly politicized phase in its history.

The origins of the Sevillian Protestant movement were discovered within the very heart of the cathedral church itself in the early 1550s. Many humanist scholars from Alcalá had been appointed to serve as preachers and theologians in Seville under the Erasmian Archbishop Alonso Manrique. They included Dr Juan Egidio and Dr Constantino Ponce de la Fuente. In August 1552, following a two-year trial, the magistral canon Egidio was found guilty of unorthodox teachings and sentenced to a year of reclusion. He was furthermore banished from preaching and publishing his work for a period of ten years. Following his death in 1556, the Holy Office began to hound his successor, Dr Constantino, a *converso* preacher and former chaplain to Charles V who had come in contact with Protestant propaganda during his travels with the Emperor through Germany (1548–53). He was an ideal victim for the 'sombre men' of the Inquisition who sought to remove all traces of religious deviance from Spain. He was tainted by his blood and his 'foreign' connections and therefore was inevitably branded a heretic. In November 1557, an 'active' cell of approximately 120 Protestant reformers of Calvinist orientation, with a fairly sophisticated network of evangelical contacts, was exposed from within the Jeronimite communities of San Isidro del Campo and

Santa Paula in Seville. Some of their leading friars, including Casiadoro de la Reina (the first translator of the Bible into Castilian), took flight before their discovery. In the wake of this scandal, Constantino was seized in August 1558 and died in the cells of the Inquisition two years later. Both he and Egidio, held responsible for generating religious dissent in the city, were burnt in effigy in the second Sevillian anti-Protestant *auto de fe* of 22 December 1560.

Another distinguished Alcalá scholar was a key member of the Valladolid Protestant cell – Dr Agustín Cazalla, son of Pedro de Cazalla and the *conversa* Leonor de Vivar, whose house in Valladolid had operated as a centre of Illuminist activity in the early 1520s under the direction of Francisca Hernández, who later defected from the group and informed on it. Dr Cazalla was a highly respected figure in both ecclesiastical and courtly circles. As imperial chaplain and preacher he was part of the same cosmopolitan entourage of the Emperor to which Constantino belonged. He, too, had travelled widely in northern Europe where he came in contact with reformist views. In 1552 he was appointed a canon of Salamanca. By 1557 he had fallen under the influence of the leader of the Valladolid group, the Italian nobleman Carlos de Sesso, who had been employed in the royal household in the early 1550s. Within two years, the whole Cazalla family had turned towards Protestantism. Early in 1558 the Inquisition was on their trail. The arrests of suspects began towards the end of April and trials commenced in May. Agustín, together with his brother Francisco, who was a local priest, and his sister Beatriz, a *beata* (spiritual devotee), were all burnt at the stake in the first anti-Protestant *auto de fe* held in Valladolid on Trinity Sunday, 21 May 1559. An effigy of their mother was also burnt at the ceremony. Another brother, Pedro (also a local priest), was condemned to death in the second such *auto* staged in the city five months later. Dr Cazalla, whose background was touched by Illuminist, Erasmian and Lutheran sympathies, was both a product of the rich and varied spiritual climate of the first half of the sixteenth century and, at the same time, a victim of the campaign of suspicion and mistrust mounted against exponents of what were deemed to be 'alien' strands of belief at the beginning of the second half of the century.

Philip II's first official act as king on his return to Spain from Flanders in 1559 was to preside over the second anti-Protestant *auto de fe*, held on 8 October in the Plaza Mayor of Valladolid, at which twelve suspected Lutherans were condemned to death at the stake, including the leader of the group, Carlos de Sesso, whose last-minute appeal to the king for mercy was refused. In the fires that raged on the outskirts of Valladolid on 21 May and 8 October 1559, the outward traces of liberal spiritual persuasion that permeated elements of early sixteenth-century Spanish society were dramatically extinguished. By giving his support to the Inquisition's spectacular propaganda exercise waged against Protestantism right at the beginning of the new reign, Philip associated himself directly with the ruthless extirpation of heresy from his realms. The rejection of 'contaminated' northern European thought and the imposition of a strictly regulated ideology from the centre served to reinforce social cohesion and a sense of national identity at a time when Spain felt particularly under threat from outside influences. By taking on the task of 'keeping at bay the enemies of God', the Holy Office imposed a model of conformity that bolstered the authority of the Catholic Church at home and abroad. The Inquisition used the spectre of Lutheran heresy, rather than the real existence of it, to instil fear into the Spanish people and to reinforce its ideological control over them. The calculated campaign directed by the Holy Office over the ten-year period 1555–65, which reached its climax in the Valladolid and Seville *autos* of 1559–60, successfully prevented Protestantism from establishing a native root in Spain. As a result, it never posed a major threat to the religious stability of the Spanish kingdoms (see table 5.1).

One of the outcomes of the Valladolid trials was that the newly appointed Archbishop of Toledo, Bartolomé de Carranza y Miranda, was compromised during the investigations. A number of those arrested, including a fellow member of the Order of Preachers, Domingo de Rojas, claimed that Carranza secretly supported the ideas of reformists. The Archbishop had also once acted as confessor to Agustín Cazalla and was acquainted with Carlos de Sesso. He had accompanied the future Philip II to England in 1554 where he had come in contact with evangelical views. While investigating heretical literature in Flanders in 1558,

Table 5.1 Protestant victims of the Seville and Valladolid *autos de fe* of 1559–60

Date of *auto*	Total number accused	Protestants accused (% of total)	Protestants burnt (% of total)
Valladolid			
21 May 1559	31	30 (97%)	14 (45%)
8 Oct 1559	30	25 (83%)	12 (40%)
28 Oct 1559	37	14 (38%)	3 (8%)
Seville			
24 Sep 1559	80	22 (28%)	20 (25%)
22 Dec 1560	44	40 (91%)	17 (39%)

Source: González Novalín, 1971, II, pp. 233–5, 260–6

Carranza had published his *Commentaries on the Christian Cat-echism* in which he attacked innovative forces within the Church but in doing so exposed himself to criticism of sympathizing with these views. Two renowned Dominicans, Melchor Cano and Domingo de Soto (both companion theologians of Carranza at the Council of Trent, but resentful of his rapid career elevation) soon found ample evidence in the *Commentaries* of Lutheran (as well as Illuminist) doctrine, leading to a fundamental questioning of the Archbishop's orthodoxy. Cano's verdict was that 'This book . . . is almost as harmful to us as though religion itself were taken away from us' (Pinto Crespo, 1987b, p. 317). These accusations gave Inquisitor General Valdés the opportunity he had long awaited to seek revenge on an old enemy. In a sermon preached shortly after entering his Archdiocese for the first time in December 1558, Carranza spoke of the spiritual malaise that existed in society. 'People call prayer, church-going, communion and confession *alumbrado*. They will soon call them Lutheran', he remarked (Hamilton, 1992, p. 108). He could not have made a more prophetic statement about his own future. On 22 August 1559 the Archbishop was arrested without warning on a charge of heresy (Lea, 1922, II, pp. 41–86; González Novalín, 1968, I, pp. 287–379; Kamen, 1997, pp. 160–3).

As his imprisonment dragged on, Carranza appealed to Rome where he hoped that his case would get a fairer hearing. Philip II eventually conceded to the transfer of authority and in 1567 the trial began again, all the evidence being re-examined by papal judges. Pius V was known to favour acquitting Carranza of the charges brought against him but died in May 1572, shortly before denouncing 'the theologians of Spain [who] want to make him a heretic although he is not one!' (Kamen, 1997, p. 161). A final 'compromise' judgement on the case was issued by Gregory XIII on 14 April 1576. Carranza was accused of being 'gravely suspect of heresy' (*vehementemente sospechoso de herejía*) and was ordered to abjure sixteen suspect propositions from his writings. He was forbidden from returning to his post as Archbishop for five years. However, Carranza's freedom was to be short-lived. He died in Rome on 2 May, less than one month after his release from seventeen years of imprisonment. None of the protagonists in this drama could claim outright victory or defeat. The Spanish Crown had been forced to concede to papal authority. The Inquisition had effectively exceeded its powers and emerged severely discredited from the episode. Although it was still capable of striking with vengeance in the name of orthodoxy, the Carranza trial marks something of a watershed in its history. Cases of Lutheranism brought before its tribunals virtually disappeared after 1580, by which time it had already begun to turn its attention to new areas of heresy within Old Christian ranks.

Inquisitorial Censorship and the 1559 Index

Inquisitor General Valdés had yet another powerful weapon at his disposal to thwart the threat that the Protestant ideological offensive appeared to represent to the religious stability of the Spanish kingdoms in the late 1550s – that of censorship. In August 1559 Valdés published the first Spanish Index of prohibited texts, modelled on that produced by the University of Louvain in 1550. As well as banning the works of Protestant reformers and those condemned by the Inquisition (including Erasmus), Valdés's Index delivered a heavy blow to some of the most popular works of Spanish devotional literature – eagerly consumed by the reading public – but whose spiritual persuasion now posed a threat to the orthodox regime. The 170 Spanish titles listed included major works by Juan and Alonso de Valdés, Juan de Cazalla, Constantino de la Fuente, Juan de Ávila, Fray Luis de Granada, Francisco de Borja, Ignatius Loyola and Archbishop Bartolomé Carranza, who as we have seen was the Inquisitor General's most recent victim. Valdés struck at Carranza's friends (and therefore his own enemies) without regard for what really constituted heretical literature. Fray Luis de Granada was a former pupil of Carranza's at San Gregorio and knew Juan de Ávila well. Francisco de Borja was a key witness for the defence in the Archbishop's trial. Intellectual and personal rivalry lay behind the repressive attack on Castilian creativity. It was acknowledged that these works were banned, 'not because their authors have strayed from the Catholic Church, but because it is not appropriate that certain theses be accessible in the native language [...] for although written in good faith their meaning might be misinterpreted' (García-Cárcel and Moreno Martínez, 2000, pp. 330–1). This led censors to be more lenient with works written in Latin (the language of the learned) than in Spanish (the language of the masses). The prohibition proved to be temporary in the case of some of the most widely read works. Luis de Granada successfully sought papal approval of his writings. By 1567, following revision and further examination, both his *Book of Prayer* (*Libro de oración*) and *Guide for Sinners* (*Guía de pecadores*) were back in print in Spain. Likewise, Juan de Ávila's *Audi, filia* was republished in revised form in 1574 following its original ban (see table 5.2).

While the Inquisition was responsible for the identification of heretical literature via the Index, the Crown took on the role of controlling the licensing, printing, movement and storage of books. A royal pragmatic was issued on 7 September 1558 which prohibited the import into Spain of all foreign texts in translation and ordered the retention of those already in circulation that were condemned by the Inquisition. The legislation invested responsibility in the Council of Castile for the licensing of all new books for publication. Commissioners were distributed at seaports and along frontiers to prevent the entry of undesirable books. Bookshops and libraries were regularly searched and

Table 5.2　Examples of prohibited works by Spanish writers included in Valdés' Index of 1559

Author	Major work(s) prohibited	Accusation
Juan de Ávila	Audi, filia (1554)	Illuminism
Hernando de Talavera	Cathólica Impugnación (1487)	Judaism
Alonso de Valdés	Diálogo de Mercurio y Charón (1529)	Erasmianism
Juan de Valdés	Diálogo de Doctrina Christiana (1529)	Erasmianism
Luis de Granada	Libro de oración y meditación (1554)	Illuminism
	Guía de pecadores (1556)	Illuminism
Juan de Cazalla	Lumbre de alma (1528)	Protestantism
Constantino de la Fuente	Summa de Doctrina Christiana (1543)	Protestanism
Francisco de Borja	Obras del Cristiano (1556)	Illumunism
Ignatius Loyola	Ejercicios Espirituales (1535)	Illuminism
Bartolomé de Carranza	Comentarios sobre el Catecismo Cristiano (1558)	Protestantism

Source: Márquez, 1980, pp. 223–35

local tribunals made responsible for the collection and public burning of all works by heretics. Readers, too, had to become vigilant. Those authors, printers or distributors who flouted the prohibitions were threatened with punishment, the ultimate penalty for disobedience being death, although there is no evidence that this sanction was applied. The publication of edicts and indexes or catalogues of prohibited works, produced in collaboration with censors (normally theologians from major universities and often members of religious orders) complemented the system of control. This apparatus remained virtually intact until the abolition of the Inquisition at the beginning of the nineteenth century. In November 1559, Philip II announced a further measure to avoid the infiltration of heterodox views into Spain: he recalled all those studying or teaching at European universities, with the exception of specific colleges in Italy (Bologna, Rome, Naples) and Portugal (Coimbra) (Pinto Crespo, 1987a, pp. 177–81).

In practice the effects that these restrictions placed on Spaniards' access to learning and scholarship proved to be less harsh
than might have initially been feared. The notion that an iron
curtain descended on Spanish culture after 1558–9 is now
regarded by many scholars as an overly severe judgement. In
mid-century Castile, most literate members of society would
have been able to gain access to the works of reformers, had
they wished to, via their travels abroad, contacts with the eastern
kingdoms (where the flow of foreign literature was subject to less
harsh restrictions) and clandestine book importers (Kamen,
1997, pp. 104–6). Although Spain was officially 'closed' to the
influx of European thought, it remained 'open' to commercial,
diplomatic and military contacts of international dimension,
which undoubtedly shaped its development. Native scholars
had to work within an orthodox framework if they chose to
publish their works in Spain, but freedom of thought and speech
were not totally suppressed. Although censorship remained in
place as a formal protection against heresy, many anomalies
arose in the application of its rules. Francisco de Osuna's classic
manual of prayer and meditation, *The Third Spiritual ABC*
(1527), an essential guide for all *Alumbrados*, escaped inquisitorial scrutiny until 1612. Fernando de Rojas's *La Celestina* (1499) –
one of the most widely read works of Spanish literature of the
period which overturned the traditional values of orthodox society – was not expurgated until 1632, and then only on account
of the author's *converso* background. Bartolomé de las Casas'
Brief Destruction of the Indies, that criticized Spaniards for their
savagery and cruelty in the treatment of the native Indian population of the New World, was not prohibited until 1660, more
than a century after its original publication in 1552. Creative
culture certainly suffered a setback as a result of the measures
of 1558–9, but not a permanent decline. Of the 670 texts on
Valdés's Index, less than 15 per cent were Castilian. European
(as opposed to Spanish) literature continued to be the
main target of Gaspar de Quiroga's Index, published in two
parts in 1583 (prohibited texts) and 1584 (expurgated texts).
The majority of the 2,300 prohibitions it contained were unknown or inaccessible to the ordinary Spanish reading public.
Subsequent indexes of 1612, 1632 and 1640 incorporated only

minor revisions where native literature was concerned (Kamen, 1997, pp. 116–17).

Biblical Scholarship under Scrutiny

Biblical scholarship came under particularly close scrutiny in the wake of the publication of *A General Censure of Bibles* in 1554 and Valdés' Index of 1559, which incorporated biblical censure. Whereas vernacular translations of the Bible from Latin and Greek had been encouraged in the first half of the century, during the second half any commentaries or editions that might distort its authentic meaning became suspect. The case brought against the Augustinian friar Luis de León in 1572 illustrates the tensions that ensued between the innovative and traditional branches of Spanish scholarship as a result of the Inquisition's censure of non-orthodox interpretations of the Holy Scriptures. Elected to the Thomas Aquinas chair in theology at Salamanca at the age of 34, Luis de León incurred the animosity and suspicion of fellow professors on account of his unconventional theological views. His avowed preference for the original Hebrew version of the Bible as opposed to the Latin Vulgate one brought him into conflict with his Dominican colleagues. His *converso* background made him all the more vulnerable to accusations of harbouring Jewish sympathies. Aware of the attacks being made on him, but confident of his own innocence, Luis de León voluntarily submitted his works to the Inquisition for examination and vigorously defended himself on all charges. Although it soon became clear that there were no grounds for prosecution, endless discussions between censors over the subtleties of his theological interpretation caused the trial to drag on for over four and a half years. 'What a miserable state is that of the virtuous man! As a reward for his achievements he has to endure the hatred and accusations of the very people who should be his defenders', wrote the Jesuit Juan de Mariana who witnessed events (Lynch, 1965, I, p. 251). Fray Luis's downfall came about as a direct result of his intellectual prowess, which was too powerful for the contemporary climate. On his release in December 1576 (eight months after Carranza's conditional acquittal), he was reprimanded and required to retract several offensive propositions made in a lecture on the Vulgate. He was warmly received on his return to the university in January 1577 and quickly resumed his academic career. When a further attempt was made to condemn him for his interpretation of the Scriptures in 1582, the Inquisitor General Gaspar de Quiroga intervened personally to overturn the prosecution.

As Luis de León awaited the outcome of his trial, a fellow professor, León de Castro, who had brought the case against him, turned his attention to defaming another Hebraist scholar, Benito Arias Montano (Rekers, 1972, pp. 40–1). Montano, a participant at the third session of Trent, had been sent by Philip II to Antwerp in 1568 to collaborate with French and Dutch scholars in the production of a new edition of the Polyglot Bible at the Plantin press. Three years later, and half a century after the original Complutensian Bible had revolutionized the reading of the Scriptures, the new Polyglot Bible was in print in the Netherlands and soon received papal approval. Meanwhile León de Castro was preparing to denounce Montano to the Inquisition for producing a work of flawed orthodoxy on account of its loose interpretation of the Vulgate alongside the Hebrew text. Fearing his own arrest, Montano travelled to Rome to plead for support from a congregation of cardinals. While approving of the new Polyglot, they refused to concede any challenge to the authority of the Latin Vulgate Bible. Montano was subsequently 'retired' to the post of curator of the royal library at Philip II's monastery-palace of the Escorial where, ironically, his duties included the classification and expurgation of suspect texts. In 1577, Mariana, on behalf of the Inquisition, issued a favourable verdict on the new Polyglot and it was allowed to circulate freely in Spain. Shortly after Luis de León was let off with a reprimand, the charge against Montano was also dropped. For all its attempts to impose a regulated ideology, the Inquisition was not always able to justify its censorship of the liberal, progressive forces that remained prominent within intellectual and religious life.

6 The Inquisition and Minor Heresy

While the primary function of the Holy Inquisition in its initial stages was to keep Spain free from the incidence of Major Heresy, from the 1560s onwards, in the wake of the Council of Trent's recommendations on Catholic doctrine and discipline, it intervened increasingly to correct the unorthodox beliefs and behavioural practices of the Old Christian, including the utterance of blasphemous remarks, acts of sexual promiscuity and belief in the supernatural powers of witches. Fifteen of the 28,000 cases brought before the Holy Office in the period 1560–1614 involved such crimes of Minor Heresy. Parish priests were charged with improving the religious knowledge of the people in post-Tridentine Spain, via programmes of instruction and correction, but their pedagogical efforts were not deemed effective enough. The Inquisition took things a stage further, assuming a high profile role in re-Christianizing Spain. Its aim was to root out the crime of moral ignorance with the same rigour as it had done acts of Jewish, Islamic and Protestant heresy in the first half of the century. Using fear of punishment as a weapon, it set out to awaken the public conscience where ignorance, superstition and low levels of morality prevailed. Any deviation from the strictest expression of orthodox belief was subject to rigorous scrutiny. In the majority of cases the excesses of behaviour now subject to prosecution were symptomatic of the naive mentality, bordering on ignorance, of the masses rather than any deliberate attempt to offend Catholic teachings. The Inquisition undertook

Table 6.1   Cases of Major and Minor Heresy tried by the Holy Inquisition, 1560–1700

| | 1560–1614 (a) | | | | 1615–1700 (b) | | | |
| | Major | | Minor | | Major | | Minor | |
	No.	%	No.	%	No.	%	No.	%
Aragón	7,985	61.8	8,039	53.5	2,244	42.2	5,959	65.2
Castile	4,923	38.1	6,963	46.4	3,062	57.7	3,178	34.7
Totals	12,908	99.9	15,002	99.9	5,306	99.9	9,137	99.9

Note: (a) data for 18 tribunals; (b) data for 19 tribunals
Major Heresy: includes cases brought against conversos, moriscos, alumbrados and Protestants.
Minor Heresy: includes cases brought against those accused of making blasphemous outbursts against the faith, and of engaging in acts of sexual promiscuity, including bigamy and solicitation, as well as superstitious practices.
Source: Contreras and Henningsen, 1986, pp. 118–19

its task with characteristic efficiency. In the period 1615–1700, some 6,000 fewer cases of Minor Heresy came before its tribunals (see table 6.1).

Religious Instruction

So great was the Inquisition's concern about the religious awareness of the people that it incorporated a test of doctrinal knowledge into its interrogation procedures. From 1565, prisoners were asked to recite the four basic Christian prayers and make the sign of the cross. From 1570, they had to provide evidence of their attendance at Mass and the frequency of their participation in confession and communion. From 1574, a recitation of the Ten Commandments was also incorporated into the test. The archives of the Holy Office are thus able to provide the historian with an important insight into the effectiveness of the Church's teaching programme. Jean-Pierre Dedieu has demonstrated that a significant change took place in the catechistic knowledge of the people in post-Tridentine Castile. Less than 40 per cent of those interrogated by the Toledan tribunal before 1555 had

Table 6.2   Percentage of defendants of the Inquisition of Toledo able to recite their prayers successfully, 1550–1650*

	Pater	Ave	Credo	Salve	All four prayers
Up to 1550	70	86	45	49	37
1550–1554	73	85	49	54	39
1555–1564	85	89	69	70	59
1565–1574	90	93	78	71	69
1575–1584	97	97	83	77	72
1585–1599	90	90	83	70	68
1600–1650	93	92	88	84	82

Note: * With familiarity but not complete accuracy in recitation.
Source: Dedieu, 1991, p. 15

adequate knowledge of their prayers. By 1575 the familiarity rate had risen to 72 per cent, reaching a figure of 82 per cent by the turn of the century (Dedieu, 1991, p. 15) (see table 6.2). A similar success story is revealed by the findings of Sara Nalle in respect of defendants interrogated by the tribunal of Cuenca on their knowledge of the four prayers over a similar period. Thirty-three per cent satisfied the requirement in the pre-Tridentine period (1544–67), doubling to 66 per cent in the post-Tridentine period (1568–79) (Nalle, 1992, pp. 123–4).

While this research suggests that a representative section of the adult population of New Castile was equipped with the basic doctrinal knowledge required of them by the Catholic Church, this did not necessarily guarantee good Catholic behaviour. The observance of the sacrament of the Mass might be taken as an example. Although people attended Mass more regularly in New Castile after Trent – a 75 per cent minimum compliance was recorded in Cuenca in the period 1564–80, rising to 85 per cent in the period 1581–1600 (Nalle, 1992, p. 113) – the evidence suggests that it was essentially a social occasion. The Bishop of Mallorca complained in 1570 that his parishioners came to Mass halfway through and left before it was finished, talking and discussing their affairs throughout! (Kamen, 1993a, p. 119.) The effects of the Christianization programme were uneven. Significant areas of Spain remained isolated from the basic currents of reform, giving rise to religious deviance.

Religious Deviance

Blasphemy

In an effort to reinforce the educational focus of the Church's post-Tridentine mission, the Inquisition sought to control the speech, thoughts and behaviour of all Spaniards. Careless or casual verbal outbursts concerning the Catholic faith (referred to as 'propositions'), the most common of which was open rejection of belief in God, were responsible for bringing many into contact with the Inquisition for the first time. Blasphemous statements (which typically included denial of the power of the sacraments, disrespect of Mary and the Saints, objection to tithe payments and the rejection of papal authority), despite their obvious anti-religious overtones, were usually uttered in anger, jest or simply out of habit and were devoid of any real heretical intent. Among the most frequently punished expressions were: 'I deny God', 'I deny the holy oil that was used to baptize me', 'I do not believe in God', 'I speak more truthfully than God/than the evangelists'. Such behaviour now incurred a fine, lashes, or, in the most serious cases, public penance or imprisonment. As a result, everyone was forced to watch their words carefully, as well as those of their neighbour. Trials for blasphemy and for the associated crime of propositions accounted for 35 per cent of cases brought before the Castilian and Aragonese tribunals between 1560 and 1614. The tribunal of Toledo took a leading role in the campaign to correct the outbursts of its Old Christian clients. Its 'success' as an instrument of social control can be measured by the remarkable decline in cases of heretical propositions and blasphemy being brought before the local tribunal after 1590: 46 cases in the period 1591–5 as compared with 256 cases in the period 1551–5 (see table 6.3).

Table 6.3 Examples of cases of Minor Heresy brought before the Toledan tribunal of the Inquisition, 1551–1600

	Propositions and blasphemy		Bigamy		Simple fornication	
	No.	%	No.	%	No.	%
1551–1555	256	68.6	23	6.2	—	—
1556–1560	230	62.8	21	5.6	—	—
1561–1565	142	49.6	20	7	17	5.9
1566–1570	193	53.3	24	6.6	77	21.1
1571–1575	137	45.9	5	1.7	45	15.1
1576–1580	103	60.9	3	1.7	61	36.1
1581–1585	110	55	6	3	66	33
1586–1590	90	56.6	4	2.5	54	34
1591–1595	46	26.1	10	5.7	17	9.7
1596–1600	28	19	5	3.4	9	6.1

Sources: Dedieu, 1986, pp. 180–1; idem, 1979d, p. 327

Edict of Faith: Diverse Heresies (adapted)

If anyone has said that they do not believe in Paradise or Glory for the good nor Hell for the bad; or if anyone has made blasphemous statements, such as 'I don't believe, I deny, I refuse', against God, the Virgin Mary, her virginity and purity or the saints in Heaven; or if anyone knows of somebody who has invoked the devil, using spells to provoke responses, mixing the holy with the profane; or if anybody has been a witch or a wizard; if anyone knows of any cleric or friar who has married or any unordained priest who has delivered the sacraments; if anybody has heard of a confessor who has made a pass at a woman during confession, provoking her into dishonest behaviour; if anybody knows of anybody who has married for a second or third time while his first wife or her first husband was still alive; if anybody knows of anyone who has practised fornication, usury or believes that perjury is not a sin; if anyone has abused or mistreated a holy image; if anyone has expressed disbelief in the articles of faith; if anyone has been excommunicated for a year or more; if anyone has despised or held the laws of the Holy Mother Church in disrespect ... [may they declare it].

Source: Jiménez Monteserín, 1980, pp. 519–25 [translated by HR]

Bartolomé Sánchez was a wood-comber from the village of Cardenete, Cuenca, who was brought before the tribunal of Cuenca in 1553 on a charge of heresy. Sánchez's part-blasphemous, part-heretical outbursts occurred following a visionary experience he had in 1550 that bore a close resemblance to an illustration from the Conception of Our Lady. Having received an unacceptable explanation of his experience from both his parish priest and local Dominican friars, he turned to religious penance and rebellion. He began to attack priests, the worship of idols, the celebration of the Eucharist, the payment of tithes and the authority of the pope. He believed he spoke for God and that his mission was to correct the injustices delivered on society by the Inquisition and the Catholic Church. While his neighbours tolerated his outbursts as symptomatic of his eccentricity, local inquisitors arrested him on a charge of heresy. The inquisitor assigned to his case, Pedro Cortés, took an unusually sympathetic approach to the prisoner and tried to correct his erroneous beliefs. But the strategy failed and Sánchez was sentenced to death for his views. He repented, only to relapse again into his obstructive behaviour. In 1560 his trial notes disappear from the record books (Nalle, 1987b, pp. 67–87).

Gabriel López (aged 31) from Galindos, near Ávila, was brought before the Toledan tribunal of the Inquisition in 1570 on a charge of heresy. His interrogation revealed that he was a man of Old Christian stock, baptized and confirmed, who regularly attended confession. He was able to recite the four prayers of the Church in both Latin and Castilian. He earned a living as a farmhand, beggar and prayer monger, frequently reciting a paraphrased version of the *Ave María* in exchange for money, in which he erroneously referred to Christ as 'Three in One'. Upon further questioning it was discovered that, while he was able to correctly identify the three persons of the Trinity, he failed to understand the meaning of the word Trinity itself. Thus he could not distinguish between God the Father, God the Son and God the Holy Spirit. For Gabriel López (and presumably for all of those for whom he had recited the prayer), Christ *was* God. This confusion had a feminine counterpart: it was common for women, in their excessive adoration of the

Virgin, to identify her as the fourth member of the Trinity. Here was evidence of how unsatisfactorily certain aspects of Catholic doctrine were accommodated in the minds of the populace. Following a period of imprisonment, the unbeknown 'heretic', López, was forced to abjure his errors in an *auto de fe* held in the Plaza de Zocodover (Dedieu, 1979b, pp. 258–61).

While we might look upon these two cases as being exceptional examples of anti-orthodox behaviour bordering on insanity in the first instance and major doctrinal ignorance in the second, they nevertheless reveal a considerable level of religious idiosyncrasy in Spanish society, despite official attempts at correction and reform. We might conclude that the educative programme of the Spanish Church did not wholly satisfy the needs of the faithful, who struggled to understand and therefore adhere to Catholic teachings. We might further question the extent to which the punitive measures adopted by the Inquisition actually served to change attitudes and behavioural practices that had prevailed over centuries.

EXAMPLES OF CASES OF PROPOSITIONS AND BLASPHEMY BROUGHT BEFORE THE TRIBUNAL OF CUENCA, 1587

Lic. Diego Gómez of Uclés, for not allowing his servants to hear mass on Sundays and holidays. When some people challenged him over this he replied that it was not a sin.

Constanza de Alarte of Castillo, daughter of Pedro Cebián, for saying in conversation with three other girls, that those who married occupied a more superior place in Heaven than members of the clergy.

Isabel García, of Santa María del Campo, wife of Juan de Moya, for denouncing the benefits of confession in front of three witnesses. Even though she confessed and was absolved of her sins she felt that they remained with her.

Juan Pérez, a cleric from Tebar, for uttering lascivious words to a woman following confession, aimed at inducing her into dishonest activity. The woman got to her feet and the priest made amorous advances towards her.

A Franciscan Friar from Valverde, for telling a woman during confession that an ignorant priest had blessed the Holy host without using the appropriate words. The woman replied that his good intentions were not enough. The friar laughed and mocked the woman for her comments. These remarks were deemed heretical.

Diego de Villanueva of Honrrubia, for telling his neighbour that he wanted to live in peace with fellow men: when he was in the company of Moors, to live like a Moor and when in the company of Lutherans, to live like a Lutheran. His neighbour replied that it was better at all times to live like a Christian.

Source: Jiménez Monteserín, 1980, adapted [by HR] from pp. 295–338

Bigamy and sexual promiscuity

Following Tridentine recommendations, the Inquisition also sought to reinforce Catholic doctrine on the sacrament of marriage and its moral responsibilities, taking a firm stand against bigamous practice and sexual promiscuity, which had hitherto been accepted forms of behaviour. It was the common belief of the peasantry in early modern Spain that for a man to engage in a sexual relationship with a woman, either inside or outside of marriage, was not a mortal sin. Thus acts of adultery and bigamy were not regarded as necessarily wrong. Prostitution was not a hidden profession nor was promiscuity an exclusive activity of the laity. In 1567 Alonso Díaz, a labourer from the Toledan village of Carpio, was forced to appear in penance at an *auto de fe* for his apparent unawareness that it was a sin to take a prostitute for payment. In the same year a canon of Toledo, Don Fernando Bazán, was accused of being a well-known womanizer (*público cazador*) and of causing great scandal by living in sin with Doña Juana de Vargas. Marriages frequently took place between close relatives in early sixteenth-century Tuy, while in late-century Toledo pre-Christian marriage rites were a common feature of the May festivals.

Trent sought to eradicate clandestine and non-monogamous marriages and to exercise much stricter control over the legitimacy of matrimonial alliances. The Council decreed that couples intending to marry were to demonstrate their knowledge of Christian doctrine prior to an official blessing of their union. Marriage was to take place in their local church, in the presence of a parish priest, following three official announcements of their intention to join in wedlock. The notion that marital status was preferable to that of celibacy, partly provoked by the licentious behaviour of the clergy, especially those in orders, was severely denounced by the Church. Following Tridentine recommendations, a general campaign was launched to reinforce Catholic doctrine on the sacrament of marriage and sexual behaviour in general. The Church instructed and the Inquisition corrected.

In the mid-1560s, following a recommendation issued by the *Suprema* in Madrid, a concentrated effort was made by local tribunals to eradicate bigamous practice. Verbal condemnation of bigamy was replaced by much harsher forms of punishment including beatings, galley service, and in the worst instances exile. Once again, Toledo took a leading role in the campaign. Within a decade the number of bigamists brought before the Toledan tribunal was reduced by 75 per cent from 24 cases over the period 1566 to 1570 to 5 between 1571 and 1575. Attention now turned to eradicating 'simple fornication'. From its incorporation into the edict of faith in 1574, it became a punishable offence to engage in licentious behaviour. A rigorous campaign to root out sexual promiscuity was subsequently undertaken by the Toledan tribunal. At its peak (1576–90) over a third of cases fell into the category of 'simple fornication'. By the end of the century less than 10 per cent of Toledan prosecutions derived from this sphere of activity, a measure of the dramatic success of the Inquisition's campaign in central Spain (Dedieu, 1979d, pp. 313–38) (see table 6.3 above). But the message took longer to reach the more remote regions of Castile. In a report sent to the *Suprema* by Galician and Asturian inquisitors in May 1585 it was acknowledged that moral laxity was not necessarily compatible with a rejection of the faith, but it had to be pursued as if this were the case:

> the peoples of these kingdoms, where among peasants and rustics there is a great lack of religious doctrine, say, out of ignorance, that when a man and a woman have sexual intercourse, and they are both unmarried, it is no sin. And they do not say this to oppose the church with any heretical intent [. . .] but in the future we shall undertake to proceed against them with severity, [. . .] for in this way they will be relieved of their ignorance, and the

punishment will have its terrifying effect on others. (Contreras, 1982, pp. 628–9)

Only the Aragonese branch of the Inquisition had jurisdiction, granted by a papal brief of February 1524, over what was regarded as the most perverse form of sexual behaviour – sodomy. In the Crown of Castile, by contrast, the Inquisition had refused to claim jurisdiction over this offence in 1509 and it remained in the hands of the secular courts. In the three mainland tribunals of the Crown of Aragón, prosecutions for sodomy totalled 691 in the period 1560–1700, peaking in the 60-year period between 1570 and 1630 when 75 death sentences were issued for the crime (1.25 per year) and 143 sent to the galleys. Labourers, shepherds and agricultural workers were those most commonly found guilty. The tribunal of Zaragoza was particularly active in pursuing the 'abominable crime' (*el pecado nefando*) as it was known, generating half of all trials for sodomy and almost two-thirds of those for bestiality in the Aragonese kingdoms between 1560 and 1700 (see table 6.4). The secular courts of Castile were even more severe when dealing with cases of homosexuality. It is estimated that in Madrid a minimum of 100–150 people were executed for sodomy between 1575 and 1640 (2 per year) and in Seville at least 100 died in the shorter period 1575–1620 (2 per year) (Monter, 1990, pp. 287–9; Fernández, 1997, pp. 480–4, 490–4).

Upon the orders of the *Suprema*, trials and punishments for sodomy declined significantly after 1625. From 1600 anyone who voluntarily confessed to the crime could not be prosecuted. Sodomites were spared from the death penalty and rarely appeared at public *autos*. The leniency of the Spanish Inquisition in this area of its jurisdiction was perhaps a product of its distaste, even embarrassment, at having to deal with such cases. Silence thus became a substitute for the shame incurred. Punishments issued by inquisitorial courts became less severe at a time when other, arguably more progressive, countries such as England and the Netherlands were routinely executing homosexuals. In this, as in its approach towards witchcraft, the Spanish Inquisition adopted an 'enlightened' policy where one might least have expected it (Monter, 1990, pp. 296–9).

Table 6.4 Sexual offences in Aragón, per tribunal, 1560–1700

Tribunal	Zaragoza		Valencia		Barcelona		Total
	No.	%	No.	%	No.	%	No.
Offences							
Solicitation	89	36	64	26	92	38	245
Bigamy	121	30	71	18	209	52	401
Sodomy	325	47	215	31	151	22	691
Bestiality	315	64	86	17.5	91	18.5	492
Totals	*850*	46	436	24	543	40	1,829

Source: Fernández, 1997, p. 483

EXAMPLES OF CASES OF BIGAMY AND SEXUAL PROMISCUITY BROUGHT BEFORE THE TRIBUNAL OF CÓRDOBA, 1564

Francisco Granados, for cursing God and saying that it was not a sin to have intercourse with one's mother as he had done.

Leonor de la Torre, the wife of Jorge Fernández, a headdress maker, who lived dishonestly apart from his wife, for saying that it was not a sin for a man to live with another woman for a fortnight or 20 days.

Pedro Rubio, a young boy, farm worker, for saying that it was not a sin for a man to go to bed with a prostitute in payment for money.

Miguel Martínez, a carder, for marrying three times.

María Cabrera, a woman in love, for saying that it was not a sin for a married woman or a single one to have a lover.

Juan Pérez, a farm labourer, for saying that to have a young girl as a lover was not a sin.

Alonso García de Villanueva, for saying that to have a relationship with a woman in return for payment was not a sin. As he was under age he confessed of his own accord.

Source: Gracia Boix, 1983, adapted from pp. 32–3

EXAMPLES OF CASES OF SODOMY AND BESTIALITY BROUGHT BEFORE THE TRIBUNAL OF ZARAGOZA, 1593

Juan de Arbica, a labourer from La Perdiguera, aged 30, for twice engaging in intercourse with a 14-year-old boy. Under torture he admitted to also having sinned with three or four asses and another young boy. Condemned to 6 years in galleys.

Vicente Caxo, a shepherd from San Martín, aged 16, for committing an act of bestiality with a horse. Admitted culpability. Reprimanded with 200 public beatings and banishment.

Gerónimo de Carranza, a preacher, formerly a Franciscan monk, from Borja, aged 43. Two witnesses, including one woman, reported that he had attempted to have intercourse with them. Condemned to three years of seclusion, to a diet of bread and water on Fridays and prohibited from saying Mass and administering the sacraments for six years.

Friar Manuel de Arbustante, master of the Mercedarian house in Valencia, for having intercourse with eight novices, unable to control his urge. (1685–7)

Source: Bennassar, 1979, pp. 353, 367–8 [translated by HR]

Solicitation

In the intense atmosphere of popular piety that characterized post-Tridentine Spain, particular emphasis was placed on the act of confession. Penalties were imposed on those who did not fulfil their annual confessional obligation. The 'penitential ethos' provided a powerful challenge to the Protestant rejection of confession as a means of obtaining God's grace, hence its promotion by Catholic reformers. The findings of Dedieu for Toledo suggest that by the end of the first half of the seventeenth century 50 per cent of defendants brought before its tribunal had confessed during the period of Lent, compared with 15 per cent between 1575 and 1599. The increased frequency with which the laity sought confession enhanced the role of the parish priest, who required a special licence from his bishop to carry out his duties as confessor. It also put his standards of morality and powers of discretion to the test. Despite more rigorous training and selection procedures, the demands of celibacy proved too great for many priests and the intimacy of the confessional led them into temptation. The problem of sexual solicitation during confession fell to the Inquisition to resolve.

At the first session of Trent in 1545 the bishop of Calahorra, Juan Bernal Díaz de Luco, raised the alarm over the frequency of solicitation in the confessional and called for harsh punishments to be meted out to those found guilty. The problem of solicitation became an obvious target for Protestant attack: divine grace was being granted by those guilty of sin themselves. It was essential to be able to remove soliciting priests from confessional activity in order to preserve both the reputation of the clergy and the credibility of the sacrament of penance, which lay at the heart of Counter-Reformation observance. The Inquisition's interests were also at stake. As part of its regular procedures, it encouraged individuals to denounce heresies via 'confessions of conscience' before their priest (who also frequently performed the duties of *comisario*). Via a papal bull of April 1561 the Spanish Inquisition acquired jurisdiction over solicitation, an offence hitherto subject to the authority of the diocesan courts, renowned for their leniency and ineffectiveness in judging offending priests and confessors. To this end, the Inquisition engaged in an organized persecution of those who brought the confessional into disrepute (Haliczer, 1996, p. 207).

CLAUSE OF EDICT OF FAITH, TRIBUNAL OF VALENCIA, FEBRUARY 1640, CONCERNING SOLICITATION

Or, whether any confessor or confessors, clerics or religious of whatever station, pre-eminence or condition, in the act of confession or immediately before or after it, or with occasion or appearance of confession, although there is no opportunity and no confession may have followed, but in the confessional or any place where confessions are made, or which is destined for that purpose, when the impression is produced that confession is being made or heard, have solicited or attempted to solicit any one, inducing or provoking them to foul and indecent acts, whether between the penitent and confessor or others, or have held indecent and illicit conversations with them. And we exhort and order all confessors to admonish their penitents, whom they understand to have been solicited, of the obligation to denounce the solicitors to this Holy Office, which has exclusive cognisance of this crime.

Source: Lea, 1922, IV, p. 103

Initially, conflicts of jurisdiction with ecclesiastical courts and uncertainties about the definition of solicitation hampered the efforts of the Inquisition to stamp it out. In 1622 Pope Gregory

XV issued a bull which removed some of the limitations of that of 1561 and strengthened the Inquisition's hand in suppressing the offence. Henceforth solicitation was to include 'obscene acts or indecent or provocative words' that could be attributed to the period before or after, as well as during, confession (either in the confessional itself or in another place under feigned conditions) against the will of the penitent. Single witnesses (of reputable character) sufficed but there had to be two separate independent denunciations for arrest and trial to proceed. (This ruling was to seriously hinder the speed and effectiveness of the inquisitorial authorities in rooting out the crime.) On average it took two and a half years to bring an offender to trial and at least a year or two longer to deliver the sentence. The harshest punishments to be inflicted on clerical offenders were confinement or exile, with associated loss of income and livelihood. The majority were fined and permanently deprived of administering the sacrament of penance; some were suspended from the priesthood altogether. Self-accusation could result in immunity from prosecution (Haliczer, 1996, pp. 56, 63–4, 85).

The Inquisition, armed with these new powers and exclusive jurisdiction in cases of solicitation, set about its task with renewed intensity from the second half of the seventeenth century onwards. The increase in trials for solicitation was most appreciable in certain areas of the kingdom of Aragón. The tribunals of Barcelona and Zaragoza both tripled the number of cases they dealt with between the periods 1560–1614 and 1615–1700. Overall, solicitation accounted for 1.9 per cent (316 of 16,024 cases) of the Aragonese Inquisition's activity in the earlier period, compared with 4.6 per cent (379 of 8,203 cases) in the later one. But not all cases proceeded to trial and punishment. Out of 603 denunciations made by women to the tribunal of Cuenca (1561–1650), involving 343 priests, only 66 (20 per cent) received a sentence (Nalle, 1992, p. 66). Of the 223 cases studied by Stephen Haliczer for the period 1530 to 1819, 36 per cent were suspended due to lack of evidence (especially during the eighteenth and early nineteenth centuries). Of those that did come to trial, 68 per cent were judged to be marginal to the charge of heresy. Where punishments were concerned, 74 per cent were deprived of the right to hear confessions, 50 per cent were sentenced to exile for periods of between 6 months and 10 years, and 43 per cent to confinement in a monastery. Just over a quarter of the 223 cases examined (59, or 26 per cent) involved members of the secular clergy, predominantly parish priests. Mendicant clergy accounted for the majority of cases involving members of the religious orders. Among these the Franciscans figured as the most high-profile offenders, responsible for a third of all accusations (Haliczer, 1996, pp. 80–1, 86).

The confessional remained a controversial meeting place between priest and penitent throughout the Counter-Reformation period. Confessors were required to probe into the most intimate personal details of the behaviour of those who came before them, while restraining their own sexual desires. At the same time many women, confined into domesticity, used religious devotions and the confessional in particular as an outlet through which they could give free expression to their frustrations and emotions. Sin thus came to be enacted in the very place where it was supposed to be absolved. Despite the efforts of the Inquisition to stifle it, solicitation continued to pose a threat to the reputation of the clerical estate in particular and the Catholic Church in general until the end of the eighteenth century (Haliczer, 1996, p. 121).

Superstition and witchcraft

Popular superstition, a phenomenon that permeated both rural and urban life in early modern Spain, also came under the watchful eye of the Inquisition. Every community had its local healer, usually a woman known as the *curandera* or *hechicera* who could provide a beneficial cure for both physical and psychological ailments. Christian prayers combined with pagan spells and charms were employed to deal with forces beyond the natural control of man. Such traditional beliefs, handed down through the generations, formed a fundamental aspect of popular culture – one that did not necessarily challenge orthodox practice, but rather ran parallel to it. One of the greatest fictional characters of Spanish literature, La Celestina, devised by the *converso* Fernando de Rojas (1499), used her powers of enchantment (calling upon the devil, aided by magical potions and spells), as well as rhetorical manipulation, to successfully unite the lost lovers Calisto and Melibea. She was typical of many whose activities involved invoking the forces of the occult without opposing those of the divine order. Lucía de Toledo, a *morisca* from Damiel in La Mancha, was identified in 1538 by a total of 30 witnesses as an *hechicera*. Using her powers of magic, she was able to menace harvests, cure illnesses and impotence and reconcile partners in marriage. She was prosecuted as a practising Muslim, the heresy from which her sorcery was deemed to derive (Dedieu, 1987, pp. 140–1). Acts of superstition involving petty magic and fortune-telling were not of major concern to the Inquisition: they accounted for 3.5 per cent of inquisitorial activity in the post-Tridentine period (1560–1614). The offence incurred relatively minor punishment.

Ritualistic practices, incorporating elements of magic, sorcery and witchcraft, in which the worship of God was abandoned for that of Satan, represented a far more dangerous challenge to the ecclesiastical authorities. Witchcraft had been formally denounced as subversive by Pope Innocent VIII in 1484, and ten years later in 1494 the Spanish *Repertorium Inquisitorum* recognized the existence of witches. The first witch trial by the Spanish Inquisition concerned Narbona Dorcel, of the mountain village of Cenorbe, north of Huesca, who was brought before the tribunal of Zaragoza in February 1498. Her reputation for engaging in witchcraft extended over 20 years. She was accused of poisoning people, killing and crippling others, avoiding taking communion in church and of being in pact with the devil. Narbona was executed as a *bruxa herética* (heretical witch) in January 1500 (Monter, 1990, pp. 255–6).

Legends about witches who cast malevolent spells had flourished in northern Spain long before the Aragonese Inquisition became concerned about them. The policy of the Inquisition towards the existence of witches was contradictory. On the one hand, it dismissed witches' beliefs as an illusion provoked by the devil. On the other, it insisted that witches should be brought to trial because their erroneous beliefs were worse than paganism and could be considered as a form of heresy (Lea, 1922, IV, p. 210). This second line of approach was adopted shortly after the publication in Spain of the *Malleus Maleficarum* (Hammer of Witches) in 1486 – the central theological work on witches – which favoured prosecution for witchcraft. Drawing upon its recommendations, the tribunal of Zaragoza embarked upon an aggressive campaign to stamp out witchcraft in Aragón while in Catalonia and Navarre no action was taken against the phenomenon (Monter, 1990, p. 257). At the beginning of the sixteenth century cases of witchcraft began to appear in the records of tribunals outside the kingdom of Aragón. In 1526, upon the orders of the *Suprema*, a special committee was set up, charged with clarifying inquisitorial policies towards witchcraft in the light of certain doubts that had arisen in witch trials in the kingdom of Navarre. The central question was whether it could be established as fact or fiction that witches went to the Sabbath in person. The final decision (with a vote of 6 in favour and 4 against) was that witches really did commit the crimes they confessed to. The winning argument was that to interpret their activities as imaginary would effectively invalidate the Inquisition's claim to try them as heretics. Despite the importance of this ruling, caution was advised in dealing with cases of witchcraft. Preaching and instruction of the ignorant were actively encouraged in place of the physical punishment and/or confiscation of property of those accused. When an outbreak of witchcraft occurred in Catalonia in 1549, the *Suprema* intervened to reduce the severity of sentences imposed and the tribunal's senior inquisitor, Dr Sarmiento, was removed from his office. Henceforth any vote to execute a witch was to be referred to the *Suprema*. Following this incident, the number of witch trials heard by Aragonese tribunals diminished dramatically. In Zaragoza only one woman charged with witchcraft appeared before a public *auto de fe* in the period 1550–1600. It was only the tribunal at Logroño in Navarre that continued to deal regularly with the repression of witches (Monter, 1990, pp. 263–7).

The wavering policy adopted by the Inquisition was put to the test in the early seventeenth century when an outbreak of 'witch hysteria' shook the remote, sinister mountainous area of northern Spain, a region that by virtue of its geography and the pagan spirit that survived within it had long harboured credulous fantasies. In 1609 the tribunal of Logroño was instructed by the Holy Office to carry out an official visitation of the Basque Provinces where 'rampant witchcraft' was reported to have erupted. Witches were deemed to be everywhere, casting spells and instigating human suffering. Rumours of the foulest deeds were circulated, including vampirism, while children were apparently being abducted by the score. The epidemic reached its height at Zugarramurdi and Urdax – two villages on the northern side of the Pyrenees mountains bordering on the Pays de Labourd, where the witch-craze was also rampant. Inquisitors were sent specifically to Zugarramurdi to collect evidence. As a result of their investigations an *auto de fe* was held in Logroño on 7 and 8 November 1610 at which 31 were accused of witchcraft. Of these six were burnt at the stake, five burnt in effigy, 18 reconciled to the Church after confession and two condemned to exile, all sentences approved by the *Suprema*.

The Zugarramurdi witch trials were staged with traditional ceremony and projected as a great triumph for the Inquisition. However, a powerful voice of discontent emerged from within the very membership of the trial jury of inquisitors. Licenciado Alonso de Salazar y Frías, a member of the Logroño tribunal and canon of Jaén, made known in writing to the *Suprema* his serious misgivings regarding the whole conduct of the witch trial. His criticisms never became known outside inquisitorial circles, a measure of the controversy they aroused. Other dissenters expressed their support of Salazar, most notably the Bishop of Pamplona, Antonio Venegas de Figueroa, a former member of the Council of Inquisition. A fundamental conflict of interest thus arose with local inquisitors on the one hand intensifying their witch-hunt throughout Navarre and Guipúzcoa, maintaining that a total of 2,000 were under suspicion, and senior figures within the Church and the State on the other expressing their scepticism as to the legitimacy of such claims. In the spring of 1611 the Council of Inquisition, under the leadership of the Spanish Primate, Don Bernardo de Sandoval y Rojas, instigated its own inquiry into the affair. The Inquisitor General may have been influenced by his reading of the *Discourse on Witches and Things concerning Magic* that the humanist Pedro de Valencia addressed to him in 1610, in which he expressed his doubts about the validity of indictments against witches, especially those given under torture. Salazar y Frías (a protégé of the Inquisitor General) was commissioned to make further investigations following his disagreement with fellow inquisitors over the outcome of the 1610 trials. Salazar began his work for the *Suprema* in May 1611 and produced the first of five reports in March of the following year. He set himself the task of assiduously collecting evidence to prove that tales of rampant witchcraft were false. His findings established a landmark in the history of the Inquisition and its relationship with popular belief. After his lengthy re-examination of witnesses and testing of the evidence he concluded that the majority of accusations and declarations made in the Basque witch trials were the result of pure imagination and false rumour, that inquisitorial commissioners were guilty of forcing confessions from innocent people and that the acts attributed to witches had never really taken place at all:

> I have not found the slightest evidence from which to infer that a single act of witchcraft has really occurred. Indeed, my previous suspicions have been strengthened by new evidence from the visitation: that the evidence of the accused alone, without external proof, is insufficient to justify arrest, and that three-quarters and more have accused themselves and their accomplices falsely. (Henningsen, 1980, pp. 304–5)

Salazar absolved a total of 1,802 cases out of some 2,000 examined, claiming that perjury and false witness had been used in evidence against innocent people. In his judgement witchcraft was mere delusion. The tribunal of Logroño had gravely erred in its actions in order to create culpable evidence and therefore justify its activities. Although contested by his colleagues, the report was accepted by the *Suprema*. On 29 August 1614 it issued its own guidelines for the future conduct of the Inquisition in witch cases. In line with Salazar's findings, it advised caution, scepticism and leniency in all investigations. The authority of the *Suprema* stood firm against the majority view at tribunal level that witches should be burnt for their crimes. Effectively from this date the Spanish Inquisition exercised extreme moderation in cases of witchcraft. An ambiguous situation therefore arose: while offences under the broad category of 'superstition' continued to be pursued with the utmost vigour throughout the seventeenth century (constituting over 17 per cent of cases brought before the tribunals of the Spanish Inquisition between 1615 and 1700), lenient verdicts combined with moderate punishments were issued in witch trials. The opposition of the established Church to witch persecutions meant that Spanish witches enjoyed much greater immunity than their European counterparts. While worshippers of Satan and the devil were burned at the stake in Germany and England by secular courts until at least the end of seventeenth century, in Spain they were deemed to be engaging in harmless illusion. In its attempt to control popular belief, the Inquisition admitted defeat and was forced to retreat from its all-powerful position to one of inactivity and non-intervention. Belief in witches survived – at least in the popular imagination – but the pursuit of witchcraft was to remain peripheral to the Spanish Inquisition's main mission.

EXTRACTS FROM THE INSTRUCTIONS OF THE COUNCIL OF THE INQUISITION ON WITCHCRAFT, 29 AUGUST 1614

1. If the witches confess to murdering children or adults, the inquisitors are to ascertain (a) whether the victims died at the time referred to by the witches, (b) whether the deaths might have been from natural causes, and (c) whether there were any marks on the bodies or any other unusual circumstances concerning their deaths.
[...]

5. If the witches confess to destroying crops, inquiries are to be made as to (a) whether the damage really was inflicted, and (b) whether at the time in question the fields had been exposed to hail, fog, gales, or frost which in themselves were sufficient to cause the loss of the crops.
[...]

7. The Inquisitors are to instruct the commissioners and the priests to explain to the people that damage to crops is sometimes the way God punishes us for our sins, and sometimes it is a natural consequence of bad weather. These things occur everywhere whether there are witches present in the district or not, and it is therefore most undesirable for people to believe that the witches are always to blame.

8. In any concrete instance the inquisitors are to make efforts to verify whether the witches really did go to the Sabbath (*aquelarre*) or in fact did not set foot outside the door on the nights when they maintain they had been to the gatherings. This can be ascertained by questioning those who live in the same house as the witch.

Continues

Continued

9. Whenever a person comes to make a confession of witchcraft or to denounce others, his entire statement is to be written down in the same words and style that he himself uses and with all the contradictions he may make. Afterwards he is to be expressly questioned regarding his motives for making the confession and whether he has been exposed to violence or coercion in this connection. If he testifies against others, attempts must be made to substantiate what he says and to discover whether there is enmity between him and those he accuses of witchcraft.

[...]

18. Since witchcraft is a difficult matter in which the judges may be easily deceived it is essential for all three inquisitors to be present when the Tribunal determines what investigations are to be made, and that all three inquisitors record their votes when this type of case is to be remitted to the *Suprema*.

Source: Henningsen, 1980, pp. 371–6

7 The Decline and Abolition of the Inquisition

The Inquisition under the Bourbons

During the second half of the seventeenth century, the Inquisition no longer exercised a pivotal role within the monarchy. To a considerable degree it operated as an independent body, engaging in conflict with other organs of government, while discharging a limited function in relation to the incidence of heresy (mainly focused, as we have seen, on the pursuit of crypto-Jews). With the advent of the Bourbon dynasty in 1700, it seemed that the Inquisition's power base would be further eroded. The whole ethos of the Holy Office fundamentally contrasted with attempts to release the country from its backwardness and orthodox mentality and expose it to the progressive influences of the French Enlightenment. Philip V (1700–46), in the tradition of absolute monarchy, actively intervened to assert the royal prerogative over the activities of the Inquisition to ensure that it confined its duties to the preservation of the faith. He symbolically refused to attend an *auto de fe* held in his honour in 1701. Philip's support for the cultural and intellectual enlightenment of his subjects threatened to undermine the supremacy of the Holy Office and, by extension, the rigid ideology and discipline it stood for. But the Inquisition hit back and continued to justify its existence by rooting out its age-old enemies, crypto-Jews, at a time when it appeared that the *converso* problem had effectively been solved. The campaign reached its greatest intensity over the first quarter of the eighteenth century. Between 1721 and 1725, 950 Judaizers (principally of Portuguese origin) were prosecuted, 902 of them by Castilian tribunals, of whom 165 suffered the death penalty (Kamen, 1985, p. 234; Lynch, 1992, pp. 152–3).

From the middle of the eighteenth century, under the new monarchy of Ferdinand VI (1746–59), respect for the Inquisition was diminishing, its workload decreasing and the numbers of its personnel contracting, although its bureaucratic structures remained intact. Edicts of faith were no longer issued and there was a marked tendency towards simplicity of procedure and lenience in the treatment of culprits. The majority of cases brought before inquisitorial tribunals from mid-century concerned 'propositions' – public outbursts against the faith – as well as the non-observance of church ceremonies or a lack of veneration of sacred images. The last person to suffer the death penalty at the hands of the Inquisition was Dolores of Seville, who in 1781 provoked the wrath of the institution on account of her claim that she made contact with the Virgin and released millions of souls from purgatory (Callahan, 1984, p. 33). The incidence of major heresy was now negligible. Judaizers were rarely brought to trial. Henry Swinburne, who travelled through Spain between 1775 and 1776, remarked that Jews enjoyed complete freedom of movement throughout the peninsula. Another traveller, the English clergyman Joseph Townsend, commenting on the state of the Inquisition in the mid-1780s, referred to it as being bureaucratically strong but institutionally weak (Lynch, 1992, p. 153).

The reign of Charles III (1759–88) was marked by a series of measures proposed by his minister, the Count of Campomanes, designed to reduce the independence of the Inquisition, to repress abuses and to confine its sphere of influence to the suppression of heresy. The policy of Campomanes, presented as a defence of the royal prerogative, led in 1767 to the expulsion of 2,641 Jesuits resident in Spain – powerful figures in inquisitorial politics. The Jesuits of eighteenth-century Spain were no longer the missionary figures of Loyola's making, but they remained influential in education and occupied a privileged position at Court, where the post of royal confessor was predominantly held by Jesuits, who were well connected in aristocratic

circles. However, the Society was not popular within the ecclesiastical establishment itself, especially with other religious orders.
But while some sectors of the Spanish Church welcomed their
expulsion, the move aroused considerable resentment from
within the Holy Office itself whose authority was weakened by
its loss of Jesuit employees (Callahan, 1984, pp. 28–9). In 1768
the Council of Castile imposed severe restrictions on the Inquisition's authority in matters of censorship. The Crown affirmed
its right 'to watch over the use which the Inquisition makes of its
jurisdiction, to enlighten it, to reform its abuses, to impose
limitations on it and even to suppress it if this should be
demanded by necessity and public utility' (Callahan, 1984,
p. 33). The Inquisition reacted by condemning works by Mon-
tesquieu, Voltaire and Rousseau, among other leading writers of
the Enlightenment, and by arresting in 1776 a leading official
and admirer of the French philosophers, Pablo de Olavide, for
reading prohibited books and a lack of respect for holy days. The
charge of formal heresy against Olavide rested on a series of
dubious allegations levied against him while he was governor of
Seville (1769–76). Although a devout Catholic, he disliked the
ceremony and outward show of piety characteristic of Spanish
Catholicism and did not hesitate to voice his objections. Olavide's view of religion – that it should emphasize interior holiness
rather than external ritual – was not significantly different from
that expressed by another generation of 'enlightened' Spanish
thinkers – the *Alumbrados* – at the beginning of the sixteenth
century (Callahan, 1984, pp. 34–5). The exaggerated words of a
popular song, which accused Olavide of being 'a Lutheran, a
freemason, an atheist, a heathen and a Calvinist, a Jew and an
Arian', encapsulated the prejudices sown by the Inquisition over
300 years of its history (Lynch, 1992, p.154). The case demonstrated how the Holy Office could still strike a blow within
enlightened circles of government and society.

Another of Charles III's progressive ministers, the Count of
Floridablanca, raised the debate over the abolition of the three-
century-old statutes of *limpieza de sangre* that continued to
divide society on irrational grounds. In a document of 1787,
addressed to other ministers, he referred to the discrimination
suffered by the ancestors of *conversos*, 'whereby the greatest and

holiest action of man, conversion to our holy faith, is visited with the same punishment as the greatest crime, apostasy, for the converted and their descendants are regarded as equally infamous as those convicted or punished for heresy and apostasy' (Lynch, 1992, p. 154). However, he failed to convince traditionalists within the Church and State hierarchy of the need to rid Spain of such prejudices that underpinned much of the practice of the Inquisition itself.

Moves to restore jurisidiction in matters of the faith to Spanish bishops, proposed by the leading light of intellectual life under Charles IV (1788–1808), Gaspar Melchor de Jovellanos, were fiercely rejected. Denounced to the Inquisition in 1794 for his allegedly subversive proposals on agrarian reform and his attack on ecclesiastical land and property ownership, Jovellanos' case was suspended due to his influence at Court. He made no attempt to conceal his hostility towards the Inquisition, which he saw as a fundamental obstacle to cultural progress. In a representation to the king of 1798 Jovellanos argued that the injustices committed against a whole section of society by the Inquisition should now be remedied. The tribunal had lost all theoretical justification for its existence since the modern threat to religion no longer came from Jewish, Moorish and Protestant heresies, but from unbelievers. Against these the tribunal would be of little avail since its ministers were ignorant and incapable. The time had come to get rid of such a superfluous body, to right the wrongs of history, and to restore to bishops their old powers over heresy. But for all this, Jovellanos, whose views were shared by other Catholic liberals, was not a radical revolutionary. His desire for reform was tempered by a concern for stability (Hargreaves-Mawdsley, 1973, pp. 185–7).

Paradoxically, the French Revolution is probably the single factor that contributed most to extending the life of the Inquisition and raising it in the esteem of many Spaniards. While the overthrow of monarchical authority and its replacement by the sovereignty of the people were being triumphed across the Pyrenees the Inquisition responded to the emergence of this new order, claiming that the institution's work was essential for the exclusion of the 'heresies' of liberty and equality. Its censoring authority was revived and enabled the conservative government to keep the nation free of subversive opposition. Although the restored Inquisition might today be viewed as an embodiment of an evil, authoritarian rule that assumed the right to pry into the most intimate aspects of an individual's life, in 1789 it was perceived by many Spaniards as essential to safeguarding the moral integrity of their nation. Many willingly submitted to its power, whether out of patriotism, fear or guilt. Anyone who espoused ideas popularized during Spain's brief period of Enlightenment was likely to be brought before one of its tribunals. As a result many liberals or *afrancesados* chose exile in France. While conservatives proclaimed religious rituals and the Inquisition as inherent features of Spain's national identity, the liberals viewed them as instruments of political coercion. However, the revived alliance between monarchy and Inquisition did not remove the tensions that existed between them. The relationship remained ambiguous, with each institution believing it needed the support of the other. Although moves to suppress the Inquisition continued to gather strength among liberal-minded intellectuals who sought to release Spain from intolerant forces, its foundations were too deep and solid to be easily overthrown. At the end of the eighteenth century, while the Inquisition remained for liberalists a symbol of a reactionary, autocratic Old Regime, conservatives saw it as being essential to the process of protecting Spain from the evils of modern thought, associated with the Enlightenment and the French Revolution. But the French overthrow of the Spanish monarchy in 1808 brought the Inquisition's activities to an abrupt end. On December of that year Joseph Bonaparte announced its suppression and the then Inquisitor General, José Arce y Reynoso, resigned from office.

The Cortes of Cádiz, 1810–1813

As the hostilities with France continued, a general session of the Cortes assembled in Cádiz in September 1810 'to establish and improve the fundamental constitution of the monarchy'. In the attempt to create a New Spain, the fate of the Inquisition, which had for so long served as a bulwark of religion, was bound to be crucial. A parliamentary commission presented a report to the

deputies of the Cortes in April 1812. While confirming its protection of the Catholic Church, it advocated the permanent
abolition of the Inquisition. The debate that ensued led to the
creation of two diametrically opposed viewpoints regarding the
role of the Inquisition in Spanish life, one liberal and the other
conservative, that gave rise to a polarization of attitudes in
nineteenth-century Spain on the future direction of their country.
Each regarded the other as the embodiment of evil, whatever the
merits of their respective positions. While clerical deputies
attacked the proposed abolition and petitioned for the Inquisition's restoration on the grounds that it protected the faith of the
people, liberal members argued that it was incompatible with the
new constitutional order. On 9 January 1813, the liberal Agustín
Argüelles delivered a powerful speech in which he denounced the
Inquisition's treatment of the *converso* community and referred
to it as an institution that had won 'the universal hatred of
enlightened man'. Another liberal deputy, the Count of Toreno,
declared that 'the very name of the Inquisition ... must be
erased from among us' (Callahan, 1984, pp. 98–9). The bishop
of Calahorra sought to overturn these radical points of view. His
verdict was that without the Inquisition the Catholic religion
would not survive.

Calls for the abolition of the Inquisition were expounded in a
powerful tract entitled *La Inquisición sin máscara* (*The Inquisition
Unmasked*), written by a liberal member of the Cortes of Cádiz,
Antonio Puigblanch, and published in English in 1816. For
Puigblanch, the Inquisition was the embodiment of all the evils
of the Old Regime, including its use of arbitrary forms of justice
and violent procedures. Instead of promoting an adherence to
the faith, it had actually given rise to ignorance and insincerity
on account of its failure to instruct and pressure to convert. It
contributed to Spain's decline by promoting war in the Netherlands, revolt in Granada, intellectual stagnation and fanaticism.
He argued that the Inquisition was basically incompatible with
progress and should be abolished without delay (Haliczer, 1987b,
524–6).

On 22 January 1813, in an atmosphere of increasing hostilities,
the 150 deputies present made their views known: 90 (60 per cent)
voted for abolition (including 32 ecclesiastical representatives)

and 60 (40 per cent) against. Spanish bishops mounted a campaign of protest, many refusing to publish the decree of abolition
(which condemned the Inquisition for its abuses and its failure to
represent the interests of orthodoxy) in their dioceses. The archbishop of Santiago was arrested and condemned to exile for his
lack of compliance in this regard. Clerics in Seville accused the
reformers of engaging in a conspiracy to destroy Catholicism and
of plotting 'to hang friars and burn inquisitors' – a reference to
the proposed reform of the regular orders, which also concerned
deputies (Callahan, 1984, p.108). The Cortes may have succeeded in eliminating the Holy Office in the 1813 constitution,
but at the price of strengthening the divide between conservatism
and liberalism in the process.

One of the most vociferous exponents of the conservative point
of view was Marcelino Menéndez y Pelayo. In his *Historia de los
heterodoxos españoles* of 1881, written to refute the works of
Puigblanch and Llorente and other critics, he portrayed the Inquisition as being at the heart of Spain's cultural identity, inex-
tricably bound to Catholic orthodoxy and providing essential
protection from contaminating heterodox views. He rejected accusations of racial and religious intolerance levelled against inquisitors, promoting instead the idea that the Jews were
responsible for their own fate at its hands. He took issue with
those who associated the decline of Spain with the activities of the
Holy Office, ridiculing the notion in cyncial fashion: 'Why was
there no industry in Spain? On account of the Inquisition. Why are
Spaniards lazy? On account of the Inquisition. Why are there bull-
fights in Spain? On account of the Inquisition. Why do Spaniards
take a siesta? On account of the Inquisition' (Lynch, 1992, p. 159).
Menéndez y Pelayo's unqualified defence of the Inquisition, written from an unashamedly 'Spanish and Catholic' perspective,
represented a flowering of right-wing political ideology that
would govern Spain throughout most of the twentieth century.

The approaches of Puigblanch and Menéndez y Pelayo, despite
the obvious divergence in their ideologies, share some fundamental similarities. They both afford the Inquisition a central role in
shaping Spanish culture over a 300-year period. From the conservative perspective, the Holy Office preserved Spanish society
from dangerous outside influences, while from the liberal one it

destroyed the potential of that society for modernization and development. However, both viewpoints present a distorted image of the Inquisition that failed to take account of the reality of its condition and function at the beginning of the nineteenth century, by which time it had become a virtually redundant institution.

The decline and abolition of the Holy Office has to be understood outside the context of these ideologies and in relation to a series of changes that were taking place in Spanish society at the time. During much of the first half of the eighteenth century Spain experienced a sustained if at times uneven period of economic growth, affecting agriculture and industry. But by the end of the century expansion had given way to recession. The decline in industrial production resulted in a rise in unemployment and popular unrest. Poor returns from the land produced a serious subsistence crisis among a population that had grown by more than 50 per cent during the century. Unemployment and poverty led to an upsurge in criminality and banditry on a scale hitherto unknown. In response to these developments, Charles III ordered the army to intervene to combat the incidence of crime, to be replaced at the beginning of the nineteenth century by an 'urban militia' that held policing responsibilities. The surge in the crime rate and increase in number of convicted criminals led to a reform of the penal system. Local judges were now able to issue a variety of punishments and recommend rehabilitative projects consistent with the severity of the crime instead of referring cases centrally through the royal courts. By the time the Cortes of Cádiz voted to abolish the Inquisition in 1813, secular crime had substituted for heresy and immorality as the major threat to the social and political order. The work of local tribunals had been taken over by an emerging rural police force. New circumstances and new institutions seriously reduced the need for the continued existence of the Inquisition (Haliczer, 1987b, pp. 534–9).

Restoration and Abolition, 1814–1834

Within a year of the vote of the Cortes and the ending of the Napoleonic Wars (1808–14), Ferdinand VII had been restored to the Spanish throne and the traditional administrative institutions of the absolute state were soon revived. By a decree of 21 July 1814 the Inquisition was re-established and with it the Church–State alliance. Its purpose was to guard against the progressive influences introduced into Spain during the period of French occupation and restore respect for the faith. The following year Ferdinand authorized the re-establishment of the Jesuits. The revived Inquisition justified its activities as censor on the grounds that it was necessary 'to root out as soon as possible every kind of publication in any way contrary to the doctrine of holy religion and to the fidelity owed to the Sovereign' (Callahan, 1984, p. 113). In the spring of 1815 a new edict of faith was issued in Madrid that singled out the old enemies of Judaism, Islam and Protestantism, as well as the supporters of enlightened philosophy. But its future as either a religious or a political tool of the monarchy was not secure and in March 1820 Ferdinand was forced to submit to liberal pressure and suppress the Inquisition for the third time in twelve years. From 1823 to its death in the following decade, the re-establishment of the Holy Office remained a major political issue. Pressure from Rome for its revival was counterbalanced by moderate opinion that sought its permanent extinction. It was left to Ferdinand's widow to make the final decision. On 15 July 1834, the Queen regent María Cristina, acting on behalf of Isabella II, formally and definitively abolished the Spanish Inquisition after 356 years of existence. Jurisdiction in matters of the faith was returned to bishops, its assets were devolved to the treasury and its employees retired from their duties. The long decline of the Inquisition prompted the satirical writer Larra to write the following epitaph in his *Día de difuntos de 1936*: 'Here lies the Inquisition, protector of the faith and of fanaticism, that died of old age' (Abellán, 1987, p. 609).

DECREE OF ABOLITION OF THE SPANISH INQUISITION, 15 JULY 1834 (EXTRACTS)

1. The Tribunal of the Inquisition is declared to be definitely suppressed.
2. Its property is appropriated to the extinction of the public debt.
3. The one hundred and one canonries annexed to the Inquisition are applied to the same object, subject to the royal decree of March 9th last, and for the time expressed in the Apostolic Bulls.

Continues

Continued

4. The employees who possess prebends or obtain salaried civil offices will have no claim on the funds of the Tribunal.
5. The other employees will receive from the sinking fund the exact salaries corresponding to the classification which they will establish with the *Junta Eclesiástica*.

Source: Lea, 1922, IV, p. 468

The Inquisition may have been abolished but the prejudices that underpinned it lived on, none more so than those embodied in the doctrine of *limpieza de sangre*. The Cortes of Cádiz had removed purity of blood in 1811 as a necessary requirement for admission to military and naval colleges, but in 1824 Ferdinand VII reversed this decree, making it a prerequisite for entry to public institutions. The Constitution of 1837 relaxed this rule but it was not until 15 May 1865 – 416 years after the first statute of *limpieza* had been introduced in Toledo – that purity of blood was legally abolished and the social stigma it carried with it removed (Lynch, 1992, p. 156). Nor did the death of the Inquisition necessarily mean the end of anti-semitism. Although religious liberty was enshrined in the Constitution of 1869, many traditional Spanish Catholics found this difficult to accept. The Jew was their archetypal enemy, synonymous with all the evils to befall Spain (*'el peligro judío'*). In popular mentality being a Jew meant not being a Catholic and therefore not being a Spaniard. The Inquisition remained responsible for generating the fear and suspicion upon which the denigration of the Jew was founded and for which Spain remained infamous through to modern times (Kamen, 1985, pp. 236–7).

Goya's Inquisition

Francisco de Goya y Lucientes (1746–1828) lived and worked through a period of great transition in the configuration of modern Spain. He served three Bourbon monarchs in succession as court painter: the enlightened Charles III (1759–88), the liberal but feeble Charles IV (1788–1808) and the reactionary Ferdinand VII (1814–30). Goya's paintings, drawings and prints provide subtle social and political commentary on Spain's changing fortunes. The images he produced in his later years project a distinct dialogue of opposition between the two ideological forces that interacted in the shaping of its identity: the authoritarian state (sometimes referred to as 'Black Spain') and the supporters of the Enlightenment who aspired to release Spain from its backwardness.

In 1797, under the liberal regime of Charles IV, Goya produced a series of 80 satirical etches, known as *Los Caprichos* ('The Caprices'), which mainly dealt with man's failings, his exposure to vices and obedience to obscure, irrational impulses that prevent him from acquiring truth and reason. In several examples, he makes both subtle and direct reference to the Inquisition as being responsible for the weight of superstition and harmful prejudices that crippled the minds of the Spanish people. Number 23 of the series, entitled *Aquellos polvos* ('Those powders'), depicts a woman seated on a raised platform wearing the traditional penitential garment (*sanbenito*) and the conical hat (*coraza*). She listens, with head bowed in shame, to the sentence read out by the judge. But Goya depicts her in light while the spectators are shadowy characters. The title refers to the powders sold by the accused to her neighbours and their harmful 'magical' qualities. The words also refer to a popular proverb ('From that dust comes this dirt'): a direct attack on the Holy Office. In Number 24, *No hubo remedio* ('There is no alternative'), a prisoner is being led on a donkey through a crowd, possibly en route to death, accompanied by two constables on horseback. Her head is held upright by a forked pole and her shoulders are exposed for whipping. She is clearly being displayed as an object of public infamy as confirmed by the jeering faces of the crowd who look on. In Number 58, ¡*Trágala, perro!* ('Swallow that, you dog!'), Goya dramatizes a Spanish proverb expressive of religious intolerance. A man wearing a penitential cap is having a syringe (symbolizing religious indoctrination) forced upon him against his wishes by a group of boisterous clerics. The background is filled with an enormous devilish figure and a monk wearing a gesture of self-satisfaction. Religious fanaticism, associated with the Inquisition, is shown as being linked to the destruction of human dignity. The etching represents a savage attack on clerics' monstrous abuse of their spiritual powers. A similar message is conveyed in Number 53, *¡Que pico de oro!* ('What a golden beak!'). A clerical seminar is held captive by its speaker – an 'enlightened' parrot – who accompanies his lecture with movements of the claw. Some members of the audience (representative of the doctors of the Church and academia) are dozing while others look on open-mouthed in apparent admiration at the knowledgeable discourse being pronounced. Human understanding and the capacity for rational thought are depicted as being debased by the folly and ignorance of the so-called educated classes (López-Rey, 1970, pp. 119–20, 144–5, 148–9).

Goya's *Tribunal of the Inquisition* (*c.*1816) (front cover illustration) depicts the Holy Office as a repressive force whose victims are portrayed humbling themselves before its judges in penance and who, via their submission, serve to perpetuate its oppressive authority. The setting is the *auto de fe*, which as we have seen was held either outdoors and attended by the general public, or indoors in church (*autillo*), or alternatively in the audience chamber of the Inquisition (*sala de la audiencia*) and attended only by prisoners, their families and officials. Here Goya combines these traditions. The *auto* is held indoors and is attended by representatives of the various monastic orders (Dominicans, Capuchins and Franciscans) wearing their respective habits. Four prisoners sit in broken poise in the foreground wearing yellow tunics decorated, according to the gravity of their crime, either with flames alone (worn by penitents who repented and were reconciled to the Church) or with flames, dragons and devils (worn by those who refused to repent). The architectural background emphasizes the notion of physical enclosure and psychological confrontation between victims and ecclesiastical oppressors and adversaries. Goya invites an antithetical reading of the Inquisition as the triumph of evil, rather than the traditional one of the ceremony as a representation of Christ's triumph over Satan. On one level, therefore, the painting criticizes the power of the institutional Church to cow men into subservience and the acceptance of its yoke by the anonymous, powerless masses. Beyond this there emerges another layer of meaning. The audience consists not of members of the general public as was traditional on such occasions, but representatives of the religious orders 'en masse' portrayed as grotesque caricatures. Alongside a pillar, an open-mouthed preacher (who might be assumed to be a 'pillar' of the community) reads with closed eyes the words of the text before him from 'blind' memory. The authority of the ecclesiastical hierarchy is thus inverted in the painting, assuming traits usually associated with the *pueblo*, society's lowest common denominator. The Inquisition accordingly becomes an epitome of ignorance rather than integrity and the people take on the role of onlookers, rather than participants. Goya turns the world upside down as he juxtaposes the highest and lowest in carnivalesque fashion and in so doing forces the viewer to question the traditional order of society and power relations within it. Beyond the grim exterior, he presents the viewer with a burlesque commentary on the institution whose authority and rituals are mocked, but not transgressed. The success of the *auto* as religious drama and dogma was dependent upon the collaboration and submission of the masses, both of which Goya alludes to in this painting (Tomlinson, 1992, pp. 166–70).

Between 1814 and 1824, in the aftermath of the French occupation, Goya produced a series of drawings, including several Inquisition scenes. In *Por haber nacido en otra parte* ('For being born somewhere else') (plate 7.1), he depicts a woman, set against a background of thick black smoke, about to be burnt at the stake. Her crime is written on the *sanbenito* worn by the victim. She is a foreign woman suspected of being a heretic. Goya uses the play of light and shadow to make his statement. The degrading punishment (exile or death) delivered to an alleged French revolutionary is depicted in *Por traer cañutos de Diablos de Bayona* ('For bringing diabolical tracts from Bayonne') (plate 7.2). Bayonne was a centre for the distribution of revolutionary propaganda into Spain as early as 1792–3. After 1814, following the restoration of the Inquisition by Ferdinand VII, severe punishments were revived for such crimes. The painting delivers a harsh criticism of both the methods and the spirit of the Inquisition. A scene that Goya himself witnessed at Zaragoza in 1808 is captured in *Le pusieron mordaza porque hablaba y le dieron palos en la cara. Y la vi en Zaragoza a Orosia Moreno/Porque sabia hacer Ratones* ('They put

Plate 7.1 Francisco de Goya, *Por haber nacido en otra parte* (For being born somewhere else), 1814–24 (The Prado Museum, Madrid)

Plate 7.2 Francisco de Goya, *Por traer cañutos de Diablos de Bayona* (For bringing diabolical tracts from Bayonne), 1814–24 (The Prado Musuem, Madrid)

a gag on her because she talked. And hit her about the head. I saw
Orosia Moreno in Zaragoza. Because she knew how to make
mice') (plate 7.3). The victim is presented to us face on, observed

Plate 7.3 Francisco de Goya, *Porque sabía hacer Ratones* (Because she knew how to
make mice), 1814–24 (The Prado Museum, Madrid)

by a hostile crowd (emphasizing her humiliation). She is gagged and bound hand and foot. Her activity as a sorceress is cited as the reason for her indictment. In *Por linaje de hebreos* ('For being of Jewish ancestry'), a long procession of condemned men, accompanied by monks and constables, pass under an arched doorway before being exposed to the public scrutiny. Goya highlights the first victim in contrast to the mass of indistinct figures that surround him. His head is bowed low on his chest in a gesture of deepest shame at the idea of having to face the scorn and insults of the mob. His crime was simply that of being a Jew (plate 7.4). The man depicted in *Por mober la lengua de otro modo* ('For wagging his tongue in a different way') is listening to the sentence being meted out to him by the tribunal of the Holy Office. He and his shadow, indicative of his infamy, stand out against the rest of the composition (plate 7.5). He is being sentenced for speaking his mind, in other words for making heterodox remarks. In *Por querer a una burra* ('For loving a she-ass'), Goya presents a simple but moving image of a man who has already been garrotted for committing the crime of bestiality and is now left for dead on a sinister stage, his executioners, inquisitors and onlookers having all dispersed. It is a bitter commentary on the inhumanity of inquisitorial justice (plate 7.6). Goya presents the viewer with the satirical image of the Inquisition as a barbaric institution that denied essential human liberties but which was in fact already fast becoming an anachronistic one at the turn of the eighteenth century (Gassier, 1973, pp. 373–4).

The Balance of History

Weighing up the balance of evidence presented here, it is clear that some of the old debates regarding the excesses of the Spanish Inquisition need to be refined and some new ones considered. The argument put forward by Lea (1922) that the Holy Office prostituted religion for material gain has been overturned by the research of José Martínez-Millán (1984). While it is true that the institution was riddled with corruption, neither the Church nor the State nor the Holy Office itself grew rich from its activities. As we have seen, the proceeds of confiscations and fines went largely

Plate 7.4 Francisco de Goya, *Por linaje de hebreos* (For being of Jewish ancestry), 1814–24 (The British Museum, London)

Plate 7.5   Francisco de Goya, *Por mober la lengua de otro modo* (For wagging his tongue in a different way), 1814–24 (The Prado Museum, Madrid)

Plate 7.6   Francisco de Goya, *Por querer a una burra* (For loving a she-ass), 1814–24 (The Prado Museum, Madrid)

to artificially supporting the infrastructure of the Inquisition and the external manifestation of its authority via the *auto de fe*. The cruelty and injustice of inquisitorial practice, highlighted by historians such as Prescott (1854), is now tempered by evidence in support of the relative fairness of the judicial process (notwithstanding its lack of defence mechanisms) alongside the infrequent use of torture and the death penalty as punishments. Recent studies in comparative history have revealed that while the level of religious intolerance exercised against Jews in sixteenth- and seventeenth-century Spain was unacceptably high, in other areas (notably in its treatment of women and slaves) its reputation was less severe compared with other European countries such as England. Clearly the 'data bank' research of Contreras and Henningsen (1986) among others does not redeem the Inquisition from its historical responsibilities. All Spaniards in one way or another were victims of its divisive influence. The debate over the extent to which the Inquisition was responsible for isolating Spain from Europe has also been turned around. Was it not, as Dedieu (1989) and Thomas (2001) have argued, Spaniards' own belief in their providential role to defend and disseminate the Catholic faith at home and abroad, embodied in a powerful nationalistic spirit, that set it apart from and in conflict with other nations and socio-religious groups, rather than the Inquisition itself that merely served to legitimize the values of the Old Christian? Other recent lines of investigation have included a closer examination of the individuals (inquisitors and functionaries) that supported the system. Stigmatized as demons by the perpetrators of the Black Legend, they emerge from the findings of modern research as career bureaucrats and clerics, some with generous hearts, such as that brought to our attention by Nalle (2001). However, the institution's reputation for inhumanity is not excused by the compassion of a select few of its employees. Was the Inquisition a mere extension of the confessional, a tool of the Church–State alliance, which instilled the notion of sin as a public crime and redemption as public service (Edwards, 1999)? Following this line of argument, the repression exercised by the Inquisition formed part of an educational process designed to instruct and to foster adherence to a strictly orthodox code of behaviour. The corollary then follows that the disciplining of sinners was indicative of the failure of the pastoral mission of the Church and the corrective role of the Inquisition. Others have argued that the responsibilities of the Church and Inquisition and their confessional functions with regard to the faithful and unfaithful respectively were quite different.

The Inquisition is increasingly being placed in the context of developments occurring within wider society, and seen as a vehicle for the projection of personal and collective tensions and aggressions via malicious denunciations. As Jaime Contreras has pointed out (1992), behind the inquisitorial belligerence unleashed in Murcia against *conversos*, there lay deep-rooted social discord linked to the failure of the middle classes to realize their ambitions. In other words, the potential for violent conflict already lay in society. The persecution of New Christians and other minority groups at the hands of the Holy Office merely provided a justification for it. According to this line of approach, the pursuit of heresy was marginal to its real function – the settlement of social and economic grievances and cultural prejudices (Kamen, 1997). While crypto-Jews, *moriscos* and Protestants were paraded as the enemies of the Spanish people, those same people were themselves either failing to meet their own obligations to the faith (and in some cases manipulating inquisitorial justice to avoid prosecution) or bringing its wrath to bear on their enemies. In this sense they controlled the institution via strategies of dissimulation in their delivery of false testimony, rather than being controlled by it via a successful programme of submission and conversion. Clearly this argument does not take account of the thousands of innocent victims who suffered, less in relation to any real crime they had committed, but rather to teach a lesson to others. While the Inquisition will never totally be divorced from the dark image that surrounds its activities nor its excesses condoned, recent research has enabled us to draw a more balanced picture of the nature and ambit of the authority it exercised, from which it emerges to pay its due penance but perhaps not to be cast before the flames. As long as the extensive archives of the Spanish Inquisition continue to be explored by indefatigable historians, so the debate will go on.

Glossary

Abogado de preso: Lawyer employed by Inquisition to support accused.

Abjuración: Abjuration or renunciation of heretical charge of which the accused was suspected. (See *de levi* and *de vehementi* below.)

Alfaquí: Muslim doctor/learned person.

Alguacil: Arresting officer of Inquisition.

Aljama: Segregated zones or ghettos in cities where Jews were forced to live.

Alumbrados: Illuminists who promoted spiritual/mystical route to union with God above an adherence to ceremony and sacramental observance.

Autillo de fe or *Auto particular*: Small *auto de fe*, usually held in a church.

Auto de fe: 'Act of faith' or public ceremony at which the Inquisition announced its sentences. *Autos* could be held for one prisoner or for several. If held with maximum solemnity in a public square, rather than a parish church, it was called an *auto público general.*

Beata: A laywoman, who took a vow of chastity and dedicated herself to religious life, sometimes within the protection of a religious order.

Calificador: Inquisitorial consultant (normally a theologian) who read books or testimony collected by inquisitors in order to assess the type and amount of heresy that was involved.

Capitulaciones: Terms of surrender of Moors of Granada to Christian rule, drawn up in 1491.

Cárceles secretas: Secret prisons of the Inquisition where the accused was held during his/her trial.

Cartas acordadas: Circulars/letters of instruction sent out from the *Suprema* to local tribunals.

Casa de penitencia: 'House of penance or of correction' where those sentenced to do penance were held.

Chancillerías: High Courts of Valladolid and Granada.

Colegios mayores: Elite university colleges of Alcalá, Salamanca and Valladolid.

Comisario: Local representative of the Inquisition, usually a cleric/ parish priest (unlike the **familiars**), responsible for taking testimony and collecting denunciations in remote parts of a district.

Consulta de fe: Jury of inquisitors and theologians who passed judgement on accused at end of tribunal.

Consultor: Legal and theological advisers who advised on the sentence to be imposed on the accused.

Converso: The name given to a Jew who converted to Christianity during the fifteenth century, either by choice or under duress.

Convivencia: The term used to refer to the co-existence of Christians, Jews and Muslims in medieval Spain.

Cortes: Representative parliament of each kingdom.

Cristaos-novos: Portuguese New Christians.

De levi: The formal abjuration/repentance by a person 'lightly' suspected of heresy; the lowest category employed by the Holy Office.

De vehementi: The formal abjuration/repentance by a person 'vehemently/strongly' suspected of serious offences of heresy.

Edicto de fe: Edict of Faith: a list or catalogue of all forms of heresy, designed to be read out in all churches after Mass on Sundays.

Edicto de gracia: Edict of Grace: a formula denouncing a specific kind of heresy and granting a period of time for voluntary confessions without punishment.

Familiar: Lay representative of the Inquisition who acted as an intermediary between the tribunal and the prisoner and whose role was to provide denunciations.

Fiscal: The chief prosecutor of an inquisitorial or secular court.

Fueros: Laws and privileges of non-Castilian provinces of Spain.

Garrucha: A pulley used to inflict torture on inquisitorial victims.

Hidalgo: Member of lower to middle nobility.

Limpieza de sangre: Reference to a series of statutes enacted in the late fifteenth/early sixteenth centuries restricting access to certain professions only to those able to prove their 'purity of blood', i.e. their Old Christian (non-Jewish or non-Muslim) ancestry, over four generations.

Maravedí: Small unit of Castilian currency; 375 made up one ducat (gold coin).

Marrano: Abusive/pejorative word (meaning 'swine') used to refer to *conversos*.

Morisco: The name given to a Muslim who converted to Christianity, but who was perceived to be continuing to practise his/her ancestral religion, as well as retaining the traditional diet and dress and the use of the Arabic language.

Mudéjares: Muslims living under Christian rule (prior to enforced baptism).

Penitenciado: A heretic condemned for lesser offences against the faith, formally 'reconciled' to the Church but obliged to renounce sins and subject to a fine, and public humiliation via the wearing of the *sanbenito*.

Potro: 'The rack' – one of the most common instruments of torture employed by the Inquisition.

Pragmática: Royal edict carrying force of law.

Prueba/Proceso: Inquisitorial trial.

Quemadero: The site for inquisitorial burnings on the outside of a city.

Reconciliado: A relapsed penitent heretic, formally 'reconciled' to the Church by the Holy Office but subject to heavy punishment, including confiscation of property, galley service, flogging and the indefinite wearing of the *sanbenito*.

Relaciones de causas : Annual reports submitted by each tribunal to the *Suprema* detailing cases concluded and *autos de fe* held.

Relajado: A heretic 'relaxed' to the secular arm to be executed and their body burned, either in person or in effigy.

Sanbenito: The 'sacred cloth' or penitential garment/tunic worn by convicted heretics during the *auto de fe* and later in public. After expiration or sentence of death, the *sanbenito* was hung in the major church of the heretic's city or home town.

Sermón de la Fe: Sermon preached before the audience attending an *auto de fe*.

Suprema: The 'Council of the Supreme and General Inquisition', established in 1483 in Madrid, under the leadership of the Inquisitor General.

Taqiyya: Arabic term meaning 'dissimulation' and referring to the tactic of false conformity to Christianity which some Muslims living under an alien faith engaged in.

Toca: A linen cloth placed in the throat of inquisitorial victims via which water was channelled from a jar.

Visita de distrito: Provincial inspection including hearings and denunciations carried out periodically by local inquisitors.

Bibliography and References

Abellán, José Luis 1987: 'The persistence of the inquisitorial mind in contemporary Spanish life and culture and theory of the "Two Spains" ', in (ed.) Angel Alcalá, *The Spanish Inquisition and the Inquisitorial Mind.* Boulder, CO: Columbia University Press, pp. 609–21.

Alcalá, Angel (ed.) 1987: *The Spanish Inquisition and the Inquisitorial Mind.* Boulder, CO: Columbia University Press.

Alpert, Michael 2001: *Crypto-Judaism and the Spanish Inquisition.* Basingstoke: Palgrave.

Avilés, Miguel 1987: 'The *Auto de Fe* and the social model of Counter-Reformation Spain', in (ed.) Angel Alcalá, *The Spanish Inquisition and the Inquisitorial Mind.* Boulder, CO: Columbia University Press, pp. 249–64.

Baer, Yitzhak F. 1961: *A History of the Jews in Christian Spain.* 2 vols. Philadelphia: Jewish Publication Society of America.

Barrio Gozalo, Maximiliano 1999: 'Burocracia inquisitorial y movilidad social. El Santo Oficio, plantel de obispos (1556–1820)', in (ed.) A. Prado Moura, *Inquisición y Sociedad.* Valladolid: Universidad de Valladolid, pp. 107–38.

Bataillon, Marcel 1966: *Erasmo y España: estudios sobre la historia espiritual del siglo xvi.* Mexico D.F.: Fondo de Cultura Económica.

Beinart, Haim 1974: *Records of the Trials of the Spanish Inquisition in Ciudad Real, 1483–1485.* Vol. I. Jerusalem: Israel National Academy of Science and Humanities.

Beinart, Haim 1981: *Conversos on Trial. The Inquisition in Ciudad Real.* Jerusalem: The Magnes Press.

Benito Ruano, Eloy 1976: *Los orígenes del problema converso.* Barcelona: Ediciones Albir.

Bennassar, Bartolomé (ed.) 1979: *L'Inquisition Espagnole, xve–xixe siècle*. Paris: Hachette.

Bernáldez, Andrés 1962: *Memorias de los Reyes Católicos*, (eds) Manual Gómez-Moreno and Juan de Mata Carriazo. Madrid: CSIC.

Bethencourt, Francisco 1997: *La Inquisición en la época moderna*. Madrid: Akal.

Bilinkoff, Jodi 1989: *The Ávila of Saint Teresa: Religious Reform in a Sixteenth-Century City*. Ithaca and London: Cornell University Press.

Braudel, Fernand 1976: *The Mediterranean and the Mediterranean World in the Age of Philip II*. 2 vols. London: HarperCollins.

Callahan, William J. 1984: *Church, Politics and Society in Spain, 1750–1874*. London and Cambridge, MA: Harvard University Press.

Cantera Burgos, Francisco 1972: 'Fernando del Pulgar and the *conversos*', in (ed.) J. R. L. Highfield, *Spain in the Fifteenth Century, 1369–1516*. London: Macmillan, pp. 296–353.

Cardaillac, Louis 1979: *Moriscos y cristianos. Un enfrentamiento polémico (1492–1640)*. Madrid, Mexico and Buenos Aires: Fondo de Cultura Económica.

Casey, James 1999: *Early Modern Spain. A Social History*. London: Routledge.

Coleman, David 2003: *Creating Christian Granada. Society and Religious Culture in an Old World City*. Ithaca and London: Cornell University Press.

Contreras, Jaime 1982: *El Santo Oficio de la Inquisición de Galicia, 1560–1700: poder, sociedad y cultura*. Madrid: Akal.

Contreras, Jaime 1987a: 'The impact of Protestantism in Spain, 1520–1600', in (ed.) Stephen Haliczer, *Inquisition and Society in Early Modern Europe*. London: Croom Helm, pp. 47–63.

Contreras, Jaime 1987b: 'The social infrastructure of the Inquisition: familiars and commissioners', in (ed.) Angel Alcalá, *The Spanish Inquisition and the Inquisitorial Mind*. Boulder, CO: Columbia University Press, pp.133–58.

Contreras, Jaime 1992: *Sotos contra Riquelmes*. Madrid: Arco Libros.

Contreras, Jaime 1997: *Historia de la Inquisición española (1478–1834)*. Madrid: Arco Libros.

Contreras, Jaime and Dedieu, Jean-Pierre 1980: 'Geografía de la Inquisición Española: la formación de los distritos, 1470–1820', *Hispania*, 40: 37–93.

Contreras, Jaime and Henningsen, Gustav 1986: 'Forty-four thousand cases of the Spanish Inquisition (1540–1700): Analysis of a historical data bank', in (eds) Gustav Henningsen and John Tedeschi, *The*

162   Bibliography and References

Inquisition in Early Modern Europe. Studies in Sources and Methods.
Dekalb, IL: Northern Illinois University Press, pp. 100–29.

Dedieu, Jean-Pierre 1977: 'Les Inquisiteurs de Tolède et la visite du
district', _Mélanges de la Casa de Velázquez_, 13: 235–56.

Dedieu, Jean-Pierre 1979a: 'Les quatres temps de l'Inquisition', in (ed.)
Bartolomé Bennassar, _L'Inquisition Espagnole._ Paris: Hachette,
pp. 15–41.

Dedieu, Jean-Pierre 1979b: 'Le modèle religieux: Les disciplines du
langage et de l'action', in (ed.) Bartolomé Bennassar, _L'Inquisition
Espagnole_. Paris: Hachette, pp. 241–67.

Dedieu, Jean-Pierre 1979c: 'Le modèle religieux: Le refus de la réforme
et le contrôle de la pensée', in (ed.) Bartolomé Bennassar, _L'Inquisition Espagnole_. Paris: Hachette, pp. 269–311.

Dedieu, Jean-Pierre 1979d: 'Le modèle sexual: La défense du mariage
chrétien', in (ed.) Bartolomé Bennassar, _L'Inquisition Espagnole_.
Paris: Hachette, pp. 313–38.

Dedieu, Jean-Pierre 1986: 'The Archives of the Holy Office of Toledo as
a source for historical anthropology', in (eds) Gustav Henningsen
and John Tedeschi, _The Inquisition in Early Modern Europe. Studies
in Sources and Methods_. Dekalb, IL: Northern Illinois University
Press, pp. 158–89.

Dedieu, Jean-Pierre 1987: 'The Inquisition and popular culture in New
Castile', in (ed.) Stephen Haliczer, _Inquisition and Society in Early
Modern Europe_. London: Croom Helm, pp. 129–46.

Dedieu, Jean-Pierre 1989: _L'Administration de la Foi. L'Inquisition de
Tolède, xvie–xviiie siècle_. Madrid: Casa de Velázquez.

Dedieu, Jean-Pierre 1991: ' "Christianization" in New Castile: Cat-
echism, Communion, Mass, and Confirmation in the Toledo Archbishopric, 1540–1650', in (eds) A. J. Cruz and M. E. Perry, _Culture
and Control in Counter-Reformation Spain_. Minneapolis: University
of Minnesota Press, pp. 1–24.

Domínguez Ortiz, Antonio 1957: _Los Conversos de origen judío después
de la expulsión_. Madrid: CSIC.

Domínguez Ortiz, Antonio 1992: _Los Judeoconversos en la España
moderna_. Madrid: Ediciones Istmo.

Domínguez Ortiz, Antonio and Vincent, Bernard 1978: _Historia de los
Moriscos. Vida y tragedia de una minoría_. Madrid: Alianza.

Edwards, John 1988: 'Religious faith and doubt in late medieval Spain:
Soria, c.1450–1500', _Past and Present_, 120: 3–25.

Edwards, John 1994: _The Jews in Western Europe, 1400–1600_. Manchester: Manchester University Press.

Edwards, John 1999: _The Spanish Inquisition_. Stroud: Tempus.

Eire, Carlos M. N. 1995: *From Madrid to Purgatory: The Art and Craft of Dying in Sixteenth-Century Spain*. Cambridge: Cambridge University Press.

Elliott, J. H. 1983: *Imperial Spain, 1469–1716*. Harmondsworth: Pelican.

Fernández, André 1997: 'The repression of sexual behaviour by the Aragonese Inquisition', *Journal of the History of Sexuality*, 7(4): 469–501.

Fernández de Madrid, Alonso 1992: *Vida de Fray Fernando de Talavera*. Granada: Universidad de Granada.

Flynn, Maureen 1991: 'Mimesis of the Last Judgement: The Spanish *Auto de fe*', *Sixteenth Century Journal*, xxii(2): 281–97.

Gallego y Burín, Antonio and Gámir Sandoval, Alfonso 1968: *Los Moriscos del Reino de Granada según el sínodo de Guadix de 1554*. Granada: Universidad de Granada.

García-Arenal, Mercedes 1987: *Inquisición y moriscos. Los procesos del tribunal de Cuenca*. Madrid: Siglo Veinituno.

García-Cárcel, Ricardo 1976: *Orígenes de la Inquisición española. El tribunal de Valencia, 1478–1530*. Barcelona: Ediciones Península.

García-Cárcel, Ricardo 1980: *Herejía y sociedad en el siglo xvi. La Inquisición en Valencia, 1530–1609*. Barcelona: Ediciones Península.

García-Cárcel, Ricardo 1987: 'The course of the Moriscos up to their expulsion', in (ed.) Angel Alcalá, *The Spanish Inquisition and the Inquisitorial Mind*. Boulder, CO: Columbia University Press, pp. 73–86.

García-Cárcel, Ricardo and Moreno Martínez, Doris 2000: *Inquisición. Historia Crítica*. Madrid: Ediciones Temas de Hoy.

García Fuentes, José María 1981: *La Inquisición de Granada, siglo xi. Fuentes para su estudio*. Granada: Universidad de Granada.

Gassier, Pierre 1973: *The Drawings of Goya. The Complete Album*. London: Thames and Hudson.

González de Caldas, María Victoria 1987: 'New images of the Holy Office in Seville: The Auto de Fe', in (ed.) Angel Alcalá, *The Spanish Inquisition and the Inquisitorial Mind*. Boulder, CO: Columbia University Press, pp. 265–300.

González Novalín, José Luis 1968–71: *El Inquisidor General Fernando de Valdés (1483–1568)*. 2 vols. Oviedo: Universidad de Oviedo.

Gracia Boix, Rafael 1983: *Autos de fe y causas de la Inquisición de Córdoba*. Córdoba: Publicaciones de la Excma Diputación Provincial.

Griffiths, Nicholas 1997: 'Popular religious scepticism and idiosyncracy in post-Tridentine Cuenca', in (ed.) Lesley K. Twomey, *Faith and*

164   Bibliography and References

Fanaticism in Early Modern Spain. Aldershot: Ashgate Publishing, pp. 95–126.

Haliczer, Stephen (ed.) 1987a: *Inquisition and Society in Early Modern Europe.* London: Croom Helm.

Haliczer, Stephen 1987b: 'Inquisition myth and Inquisition history: The abolition of the Holy Office and the development of Spanish political ideology', in (ed.) Angel Alcalá, *The Spanish Inquisition and the Inquisitorial Mind.* Boulder, CO: Columbia University Press, pp. 523–46.

Haliczer, Stephen 1990: *The Inquisition in the Kingdom of Valencia (1478–1834).* Berkeley, Los Angeles and Oxford: University of California Press.

Haliczer, Stephen 1991: 'The Jew as witch: Displaced aggression and the myth of the Santo Niño de La Guardia', in (eds) M. E. Perry and A. J. Cruz, *Cultural Encounters. The Impact of the Inquisition in Spain and the New World.* Berkeley, Los Angeles and Oxford: University of California Press, pp. 146–56.

Haliczer, Stephen 1996: *Sexuality in the Confessional. A Sacrament Profaned.* Oxford: Oxford University Press.

Hamilton, Alastair 1992: *Heresy and Mysticism in Sixteenth-century Spain.* Cambridge: James Clark.

Hargreaves-Mawdsley, W. N. 1973: *Spain under the Bourbons, 1700–1823.* London and Basingstoke: Macmillan.

Harvey, L. P. 1990: *Islamic Spain, 1250 to 1500.* Chicago and London: University of Chicago Press.

Henningsen, Gustav 1980: *The Witches' Advocate. Basque Witchcraft and the Spanish Inquisition (1609–1614).* Reno: University of Nevada Press.

Hillgarth, J. N. 1976–78: *The Spanish Kingdoms, 1250–1516.* 2 vols. Oxford: Clarendon Press.

Hordes, Stanley, M. 1991: 'The Inquisition and the Crypto-Jewish community in colonial New Spain and New Mexico', in (eds) M. E. Perry and A. J. Cruz, *Cultural Encounters. The Impact of the Inquisition in Spain and the New World.* Berkeley, Los Angeles and Oxford: University of California Press, pp. 207–17.

Hroch, Miroslav and Skybová, Anna 1990: *Ecclesia Militans: The Inquisition.* Wincanton: Dorset Press.

Huertas, Pilar, Miguel, and Jesús de, Sánchez, Antonio 2003: *La Inquisición. Tribunal contra los delitos de fe.* Madrid: Libsa.

Jiménez Monteserín, Miguel 1980: *Introducción a la Inquisición española. Documentos básicos para el estudio del Santo Oficio.* Madrid: Editora Nacional.

Jones, John A. 1997: '*Fervor sin fanatismo*: Pedro de Valencia's Treatise on the *Moriscos*', in (ed.) Lesley K. Twomey, *Faith and Fanaticism in Early Modern Spain*. Aldershot: Ashgate Publishing, pp. 159–74.

Kamen, Henry 1965: 'Confiscations in the economy of the Spanish Inquisition', *Economic History Review*, 18: 511–25.

Kamen, Henry 1985: *Inquisition and Society in Spain in the Sixteenth and Seventeenth Centuries*. Bloomington: Indiana University Press.

Kamen, Henry 1992: 'The Expulsion: Purpose and consequences', in (ed.) Elie Kedourie, *Spain and the Jews: The Sephardi Experience, 1492 and After*. London: Thames and Hudson, pp. 74–91.

Kamen, Henry 1993a: *The Phoenix and the Flame. Catalonia and the Counter-Reformation*. New Haven and London: Yale University Press.

Kamen, Henry 1993b: 'A crisis of conscience in Golden Age Spain: The Inquisition against *Limpieza de Sangre*', in Kamen, *Crisis and Change in Early Modern Spain*. Aldershot: Variorum, Article VII, pp. 1–27.

Kamen, Henry 1997: *The Spanish Inquisition: An Historical Revision*. New Haven and London: Yale University Press.

Kedourie, Elie (ed.) 1992: *Spain and the Jews: The Sephardi Experience, 1492 and After*. London: Thames and Hudson.

Kinder, Gordon A. 1992: 'Spain', in (ed.) Andrew Pettegree, *The Early Reformation in Europe*. Cambridge: Cambridge University Press, pp. 215–37.

Kinder, Gordon A. 1997: 'Spain's little-known "Noble Army of Martyrs" and the Black Legend', in (ed.) Lesley K. Twomey, *Faith and Fanaticism in Early Modern Spain*. Aldershot: Ashgate Publishing, pp. 61–83.

Lapeyre, Henri 1986: *Geografía de la España Morisca*. Valencia: Diputació Provincial de Valencià.

Lea, Henry Charles 1922: *A History of the Inquisition of Spain*. 4 vols. London and New York: Macmillan.

Lea, Henry Charles 1968: *The Moriscos of Spain. Their Conversion and Expulsion*. Westport, CT: Greenwood Press.

Liss, Peggy K. 1992: *Isabel the Queen. Life and Times*. New York and Oxford: Oxford University Press.

López-Rey, José 1970: *Goya's Caprichos*. Vol.1. Westport, CT: Greenwood Press.

Lovett, Albert W. 1986: *Early Habsburg Spain, 1517–1598*. Oxford: Oxford University Press.

Lynch, John 1965–69: *Spain under the Habsburgs, 1516–1700*. 2 vols. Oxford: Blackwell.

Lynch, John 1989: *Bourbon Spain, 1700–1808*. Oxford: Blackwell.

Lynch, John 1992: 'Spain after the expulsion', in (ed.) Elie Kedourie, *Spain and the Jews: The Sephardi Experience, 1492 and After*. London: Thames and Hudson, pp. 140–61.

Llorente, Juan Antonio 1980: *Historia crítica de la Inquisición española*. 4 vols. Madrid: Ediciones Hiperón [first published 1817].

MacKay, Angus 1972: 'Popular movements and pogroms in fifteenth century Castile', *Past and Present*, 55: 33–67.

Maltby, William S. 1971: *The Black Legend in England. The Development of Anti-Spanish Sentiment, 1558–1660*. Durham, NC: Duke University Press.

Márquez, Antonio 1980: *Literatura e Inquisición en España (1478–1834)*. Madrid: Taurus Ediciones.

Martínez-Millán, José 1984: *La Hacienda de la Inquisición (1478–1700)*. Madrid: CSIC.

Martínez-Millán, José 1987: 'Structures of inquisitorial finance', in (ed.) Angel Alcalá, *The Spanish Inquisition and the Inquisitorial Mind*. Boulder, CO: Columbia University Press, pp. 159–76.

Martínez-Millán, José 1993: 'Estructura de la Hacienda de la Inquisición', in (eds) J. Pérez Villanueva and B. Escandell Bonet, *Historia de la Inquisición en España y América*. Madrid: Biblioteca de Autores Cristianos, vol. II, pp. 885–1076.

Martínez-Millán, José 1994: 'En busca de la ortodoxia: El inquisidor general Diego de Espinosa', in (ed.) J. Martínez-Millán, *La corte de Felipe II*. Madrid: Alianza, pp. 189–228.

Martínez-Millán, José and Sánchez Rivilla, Teresa 1984: 'El Consejo de la Inquisición', *Hispania Sacra*, xxxvi: 71–123.

Menéndez y Pelayo, Marcelino 1992: *Historia de los heterodoxos españoles*. 3 vols. Madrid: CSIC.

Monter, William 1983: *Ritual, Myth and Magic in Early Modern Europe*. Brighton: The Harvester Press.

Monter, William 1990: *Frontiers of Heresy: The Spanish Inquisition from the Basque Lands to Sicily*. Cambridge: Cambridge University Press.

Nalle, Sara T. 1987a: 'Inquisitors, priests and the people during the Catholic Reformation in Spain', *Sixteenth Century Journal*, 18: 557–87.

Nalle, Sara T. 1987b: 'Popular religion in Cuenca on the eve of the Catholic Reformation', in (ed.) Stephen Haliczer, *Inquisition and Society in Early Modern Europe*. London: Croom Helm, pp. 67–87.

Nalle, Sara T. 1992: *God in La Mancha. Religious Reform and the People of Cuenca, 1500–1650*. Baltimore: Johns Hopkins University Press.

Nalle, Sara T. 2001: *Mad for God: Bartolomé Sánchez, the Secret Messiah of Cardenete*. Charlottesville and London: University Press of Virginia.

Netanyahu, Benzion 1995: *The Origins of the Inquisition in Fifteenth Century Spain*. New York: Random House.

Pérez, Joseph 2003: *Breve Historia de la Inquisición en España*. Barcelona: Crítica.

Pérez Villanueva, Joaquín (ed.) 1980: *La Inquisición española. Nueva visión, nuevos horizontes*. Madrid: Siglo Veintiuno.

Pérez Villanueva, Joaquín and Escandell Bonet, Bartolomé (eds) 1984–2000: *Historia de la Inquisición en España y América*. 3 vols. Madrid: Biblioteca de Autores Cristianos.

Perry, Mary Elizabeth and Cruz, Anne J. (eds) 1991: *Cultural Encounters. The Impact of the Inquisition in Spain and the New World*. Berkeley, Los Angeles and Oxford: University of California Press.

Pinto Crespo, Virgilio 1987a: 'Thought control in Spain', in (ed.) Stephen Haliczer, *Inquisition and Society in Early Modern Europe*. London: Croom Helm, pp. 171–88.

Pinto Crespo, Virgilio 1987b: 'Censorship: A system of control and an instrument of action', in (ed.) Angel Alcalá, *The Spanish Inquisition and the Inquisitorial Mind*. Boulder, CO: Columbia University Press, pp. 303–20.

Prescott, William Hickling 1854: *History of the Reign of Ferdinand and Isabella the Catholic*. London: R. Bentley.

Rawlings, Helen 1997: 'A new history of the Spanish Inquisition', *The Historian*, 56: 30–3.

Rawlings, Helen 2002: *Church, Religion and Society in Early Modern Spain*. Basingstoke: Palgrave.

Rekers, Bernard 1972: *Benito Arias Montano (1527–98)*. London: Warburg Institute.

Rodríguez Salgado, M. J. 1988: *The Changing Face of Empire. Charles V, Philip II and Habsburg Authority, 1551–1559*. Cambridge: Cambridge University Press.

Ruiz, Teofilo F. 2001: *Spanish Society, 1400–1600*. Harlow: Pearson Education Ltd.

Sicroff, Albert A. 1985: *Los estatutos de limpieza de sangre. Controversias entre los siglos xv y xvii*. Madrid: Taurus.

Suárez Fernández, Luis 1964: *Documentos acerca de la expulsión de los Judíos*. Valladolid: CSIC.

Tellechea Idígoras, José Ignacio 1968: *El Arzobispo Carranza y su tiempo*. 2 vols. Madrid: Guadarrama.

Thomas, Werner 2001: *La represión del protestantismo en España, 1517–1648*. Leuven: Leuven University Press.

Tomlinson, Janis A. 1992: *Goya in the Twilight of the Enlightenment*. New Haven and London: Yale University Press.

Twomey, Lesley K. (ed.) 1997: *Faith and Fanaticism in Early Modern Spain*. Aldershot: Ashgate.

Williams, Patrick 1990: 'A Jewish Councillor of Inquisition? Luis de Mercado, the Statutes of *Limpieza de Sangre* and the politics of vendetta (1598–1601)', *Bulletin of Hispanic Studies*, lxvii: 253–64.

Wolff, Philippe 1971: 'The 1391 pogrom in Spain: Social crisis or not?', *Past and Present*, 50: 4–18.

Woodward, Geoffrey 1997: *Spain in the Reigns of Isabella and Ferdinand, 1474–1516*. London: Hodder and Stoughton.

Yerushalmi, Yosef Hayim 1971: *From Spanish Court to Italian Ghetto*. New York and London: Columbia University Press.

Index